Questioning Numbers

Questioning Numbers

How to Read and Critique Research

KARIN GWINN WILKINS
THE UNIVERSITY OF TEXAS AT AUSTIN

New York   Oxford
OXFORD UNIVERSITY PRESS
2011

Oxford University Press, Inc., publishes works that further Oxford University's
objective of excellence in research, scholarship, and education.

Oxford New York
Auckland   Cape Town   Dar es Salaam   Hong Kong   Karachi
Kuala Lumpur   Madrid   Melbourne   Mexico City   Nairobi
New Delhi   Shanghai   Taipei   Toronto

With offices in
Argentina   Austria   Brazil   Chile   Czech Republic   France   Greece
Guatemala   Hungary   Italy   Japan   Poland   Portugal   Singapore
South Korea   Switzerland   Thailand   Turkey   Ukraine   Vietnam

Copyright © 2011 by Oxford University Press, Inc.

Published by Oxford University Press, Inc.
198 Madison Avenue, New York, New York 10016
http://www.oup.com

Oxford is a registered trademark of Oxford University Press

Library of Congress Cataloging-in-Publication Data

Wilkins, Karin Gwinn, 1962-
    Questioning numbers : how to read and critique research / Karin G. Wilkins.
       p. cm.
    Includes bibliographical references.
    ISBN 978-0-19-974739-9
    1. Political statistics.   2. Political science—Methodology.   I. Title.
JA71.7.W55 2012
320.072'7—dc22   2010021290

CONTENTS

PREFACE

The purpose of this book is to offer a primer on how to read and critique research that uses numbers in the course of empirical argument. As a supplement to more comprehensive research texts, this book should contribute toward a more critical education of students and scholars interested in the politics of research across the social sciences. This book offers not only a list of guidelines to consider in reading research, but also a critical approach to how we can best judge and use numbers in navigating and changing our social worlds.[1] In the first chapter, this approach to research is explained. Offering questions that can be posed in reading research, subsequent chapters consider how to read and critique research contexts; research design; sampling strategies; definitions; research implementation; and data analysis and interpretation. These questions are offered more as a guide than as a comprehensive checklist and are reviewed in the final chapter. Rather than naively accepting or flatly rejecting numbers, we can pose questions that will help us understand the nature of how these communicative codes have been created and how they might be interpreted, given the research context.

This critical guide is designed to aid in the process of reading research that uses numbers. Research using numbers tends to be structured in presentation along fairly conventional lines, posing and justifying research questions in an introduction, followed by an explanation of theoretical foundations and existing literature. Methodological approaches typically follow, describing research designs, sampling, data sources, and implementation procedures. Analyses then may offer descriptive assessments of key variables as well as explanatory discussions of patterns across variables in a results section, prior to broader interpretations offered in a concluding statement.

In the second chapter, the first set of questions suggests beginning with the research context, toward understanding why the research was conducted. The research context includes identifying not only the institutional affiliations of the researchers themselves, but also the sources of funding for the project. In addition, the people and organizations granting permission for the research, through access to data or through institutional reviews of ethical procedures, represent a critical part of this context. Identifying the research, funding, and other communities pertinent to the research process helps set the stage for understanding the research purpose, which then guides the paramount articulation of the research questions. At heart we need to understand how the research is justified, in terms of its social significance as well as its potential contribution to scholarship. This chapter concludes with examples of counting people participating in public protests, mortality estimates in Iraq, and corporate-funded research on pesticides, to illustrate the ways in which research contexts matter.

Following an exposition of theory and literature, most research presentations of this genre next describe methodological approaches, referring to research design, sampling strategies, and data implementation processes. Chapter 3 addresses what we can know given the research design employed. Threats to internal validity refer to specific design features inherent in experimental, quasi-experimental cross-sectional and longitudinal, as well as case study research designs. In this chapter, we consider these concerns in relation to specific research designs. Evaluations of communication campaigns are offered to exemplify the limitations of particular designs and the political implications of these decisions.

Still considering methodological approaches, Chapter 4 calls into question who or what is being studied. The subject of the research might be focused on people, as individuals or as members of groups or organizations, or on social artifacts, such as documents or other mediated or manufactured items. Once the sources of data for these subjects have been identified, we can assess the sampling strategies used to select data for the study. The nature of the sample, whether selected through probability or non-probability methods, describes not only specifically whom the research is about, but also implies to whom the research might be generalized. Threats to external validity, in terms of people, place, and time, will be considered in this chapter as well. The political consequences of differing methods of enumerating homelessness in the United States, as well as of selecting respondents for different telephone surveys, are explored in conclusion.

Building on an understanding of the source of data for the study, the next chapter questions what the research is about. Based on the identified research questions, key concepts can be identified. How these terms become defined, in theory as well as through research practice, needs to be carefully thought through. Subsequent measurement depends on how each term is conceptualized and each variable operationalized. Following a review of the political implications of variable measurement, we consider how to assess the quality of measures, in terms of their validity, reliability, and precision. How definitions matter is illustrated through examples such as defining violence, homelessness, political participation, and rape.

The research implementation is questioned in Chapter 6. Researchers might gather data through their observations of people or artifacts, or through asking questions in a variety of ways. This chapter contrasts different methods used to solicit information from people, including observations, interviews (individual and group), and surveys. How questions are asked, and the types of categories used to structure responses, is of critical importance. How researchers gain access to their research subjects, whether objects or people, needs to be understood as well, in terms of potential ethical concerns as well as potential limitations to results. Ethical issues such as how researchers might deceive, inform, and convince research participants, in public as well as private spaces, are considered. This chapter also questions how researchers document their observations for analysis. Research on political attitudes and engagement, beliefs about rape, and estimates of homelessness illustrate the critical impact of implementation decisions on research results.

The next chapter raises issues with the analysis and interpretation of research results. Once patterns can be established in data analyses and questioned in terms of their visual and verbal presentation, assessments of strength and significance can be made. Causality is questioned as a set of conditions as well as a political need. Next, questions explore how to make sense of research results, through the process of interpretation. Interpretations help guide our understanding of what we know as a result of research. We also need to question what other alternative explanations might account for the findings, what else needs to be known, and how else that subject might be studied. How analysis and interpretation contribute to debates on effects of mediated violence, intelligent design, and political indoctrination in college serve as examples. A final chapter summarizes the central guidelines for questions to ask in reading research. How the political context contributes to the implementation and use of research then becomes a central contribution to the process of critiquing research. A glossary following this last chapter reviews central terms pertinent to research critique.

In conclusion, these chapters illustrate how research context, design, selection, definition, implementation, analysis, and interpretation matter in our understanding of numbers as political constructions. The final sections of each chapter review the central questions posed as well as key terms, followed by reflection questions and exercises. The review questions can be applied to critical assessments of research projects. The reflection questions and exercises can be used to inform discussions addressing the central issues in each chapter.

Note

1. This approach builds on Joel Best's (2001) insightful explanation of the importance of neither naively accepting nor blatantly condemning statistics, but instead promoting a critical approach to understanding their creation and use.

ACKNOWLEDGMENTS

After many years of teaching, reviewing, and conducting research, I am grateful for this opportunity to share my thoughts regarding the importance of having a critical perspective on how numbers are generated and used to advance and resist political arguments. Through my work I hope to build a movement toward numerical literacy as a necessary expertise for engaging in serious and sustained social change.

Many people have been instrumental and supportive in helping me succeed in shaping the ideas that form this book project. My father, Donald Monroe Wilkins, taught me from an early age to respect the integrity of the research process. I owe to him my appreciation for ethical considerations that strengthen the utility of research. I want to thank my husband, Paul Rubin, for his steadfast support and thoughtful interest in my work. My children, Kari and Alex, continue to inspire me to work to educate on the nature of evidence and argument.

Although I have taken many research courses, Robert Hornik stands out as the most influential of professors in inspiring me to love the art of creating and interpreting numbers. I still rely on the careful, systematic approach to the logic of research he taught me more than twenty years ago. As a graduate student I was also quite fortunate to work with Klaus Krippendorff, whose insightful grounding in epistemology helped shape the philosophical framework of my understanding of numbers. Recognizing the political significance of research was guided by my work with Oscar Gandy, whose own recent publications reinforce the point that numbers do matter in the course of political argument. In addition to my instructors, I thank the dozens of classes of research students, who have discussed with me the concepts articulated in this book.

This book has been in the works for many years, since I was first inspired by hearing Richard Rorty speak at the Chinese University of Hong Kong in the mid 1990s on his ideas concerning the philosophy of language. While I appreciated this argument in terms of the articulation of words, I was concerned that there was not enough understanding of how numbers, too, needed to be understood as communicative symbols. When I presented my early thoughts on how numbers needed to be understood as intersubjective codes to the International Communication Association Conference in 1994, I experienced the only angry response I have ever received in thirty years of conference proceedings. At that point I knew I wanted to develop these ideas further. Helping me to do so, Tom Schatz put me in touch with Peter Labella at Oxford University Press to work on this project. I warmly acknowledge Peter for his immense patience and thoughtful guidance. He orchestrated a rather intensive review process. I want to thank the many reviewers for their thoughtful comments and suggestions, which guided final revisions. These reviewers were identified at the end of the process as:

James David Ballard, *California State University, Northridge*
Bryan E. Denham, *Clemson University*
Joseph Graf, *American University*
Larry Gross, *University of Southern California*
Andrea Lambert, *Northern Kentucky University*
Dominic Lasorsa, *University of Texas at Austin*
Cecilia Menjivar, *Arizona State University*
David M. Rhea, *Governors State University*
Mihye Seo, *University at Albany, State University of New York*
Brant Short, *Northern Arizona University*
Gonzalo R. Soruco, *University of Miami, Coral Gables*
Don W. Stacks, *University of Miami*
Michele M. Strano, *Bridgewater College*
Charles Whitney, *University of California, Riverside*
A. Kathleen Wilcox, *Lewis-Clark State College*

Questioning Numbers

CHAPTER 1

How to Read and Critique Research

Who supports U.S. military intervention in Iraq? Public opinion polls range widely within the United States, from 30 to 47 percent, and across coalition countries, with opposition in Denmark at 48 percent compared with 60 percent in Italy; when Iraqis are asked, 70 percent favor military withdrawal.[1]

How many Americans can be categorized as homeless? Estimates vary greatly, from 2.3 to 3.5 million.[2]

How large is the Arab-American community? While the U.S. Census (2000) estimates 1.2 million, advocacy and commercial organizations speculate as high as 3 to 5 million.[3]

In these examples, numbers hold **symbolic value** (to articulate identity or to justify or oppose military intervention) as well as **instrumental value** (to plan for needed social services). Yet numbers themselves are constructed through institutions with their own agendas, calling upon research to legitimate their interests and actions. It is critical that we understand how to read and critique numbers as an integral part of our civic engagement, in order to pursue informed dialogue and thoughtful action.

Numbers are often posed as truth, asserted as evidence to support particular arguments. Within a cultural context that privileges science as a form of knowing, numbers are seen as a superior representation in comparison to other symbolic codes. The way we interpret and make sense of numbers depends on the context in which we live. Understanding how these numbers are created and used to support political arguments helps us question central issues in our society. As long as central political, economic, educational, and other institutions rely on numbers to validate their positions, we must have an informed community, versed in **numerical literacy**, able to critique and make thoughtful decisions.

The underlying concept here is that numerical literacy engages a language, with vocabulary and grammatical structures that serve as general rules within a research game. These rules shift over context and over time, but need to be understood in order to engage in critique. Step by step, this book goes through how these rules are used in the research process. Before considering the questions we raise in our critiques of research, it is important to have a general understanding of the underlying epistemological foundation as well as political context for creating, interpreting, and using numbers.

Understanding Numbers

Numbers are popular codes within academic and popular discourse, holding both instrumental and symbolic value. We can count the number of people evacuated from an area due to a hurricane: this number holds instrumental value, allowing organizations to plan resources to assist hurricane victims; but the number also holds symbolic value, signifying a group experiencing devastating trauma. Numbers can represent the instrumental counting of people protesting a particular event; but this number also represents the symbolic convergence, and consequently legitimacy, of a community acting collectively on an issue. Given these functions, numbers serve to communicate authority, and to establish legitimacy.

Numbers may be offered as "facts" in the course of political argumentation. This understanding builds on the idea that expertise is based in a scientific process of knowing. However, we can use numbers in research without assuming that they represent an objective reality, superior to other ways of understanding our world. What these numbers themselves represent is in question: some assume that they represent facts, as **objective** truth, others that they function as **subjective** accounts, and still others that these are determined through political and social processes, as **inter-subjective** realities shared and negotiated through communication. In the first instance, the number itself becomes a fact, not to be questioned, given its status as truth. The "truth" value of a number can be questioned, though, when many different estimations are possible, such as different ways of enumerating the number of people protesting, or the number of people evacuating an area. One response to these discrepancies may be that there are different subjective views on similar issues: people see and count things differently. However, groups can agree on numerical estimates. The position articulated in this book is that there are inter-subjective processes, meaning collectively agreed-upon perspectives, that contribute to the creation and interpretation of numbers.

Typically, quantitative research is presented as a form of inquiry in which scholars seek an objective truth, through their skill in design and precision in instrumentation; this approach tends to be juxtaposed with qualitative research, framed as an interpretive or subjective method of investigation. This "false dichotomy" between qualitative and quantitative, characterizing research as simply either verbal or numerical (along with similarly problematic black/white divides such as subjective/objective, inductive/deductive, understanding/explanation, descriptive/predictive) hurts rather than helps our understanding of research.

One critical premise of quantitative empirical investigation holds that created data should be seen as equivalent across research subjects. For example, the experience of watching two hours of television should function in similar ways for all respondents in a study. Critics are quick to assert, with empirical evidence, the fallacy of this assumption. Careful observers depict the contextual circumstances conditioning the experience of television viewing.[4] Another example that provides an easy target for criticism is the measurement of income. To assume that a numerical value associated with income would be similar for all respondents would be to ignore salient contextual factors, such as geographical region and urbanity: thus, the same numerical value may have different functional meanings depending upon the context in which the measured value is situated. Yet to critique the assumption of the functional equivalence of meaning in quantitative research is not to dismiss the use of numbers as a methodological tool. An empirical scholar can incorporate these significant contextual factors into a thoughtful interpretation.

Research represents one way to know something. Other ways we might come to know about our world might involve engaging personal experience, talking with others, and observing media. We might attempt to capture our observations through research, using techniques such as interviews, photographs, or film. What makes the research process distinct, as a method of knowing, involves the particular ways through which we learn about something. This epistemological foundation guides the process of research.

Deductive and Inductive Processes

The social science approach tends to assume that researchers engage in a deductive process; however, how we do research is more complex. Deduction involves a process through which we begin with theoretical ideas, create questions and then hypotheses, and observe and interpret data. Conversely, an **inductive process** is meant to begin with the collection of data, from which the researcher builds theoretical meanings. For example, a researcher might move deductively beginning with a theory of television and its effect on violence, conducting research based on specific hypotheses, such as stating that those who watch more television are more likely to be desensitized to violence than those who watch less. Or, a researcher might witness a crowd leaving a movie theater after having seen a violent film, smashing store windows along the way; the researcher might build toward a theory inductively based on this observation. In actual practice, research uses both deductive and inductive processes. Instead of assuming that one method of knowing is superior, we can recognize that each process has its advantages and disadvantages, and more importantly that these processes are complementary. The act of interpretation engages inductive and deductive processes, working through a language of numbers.

Intrinsic Value

As symbolic codes, numbers are created and understood in similar ways as verbal codes. Philosophers of language highlight the construction of social meaning through verbal language, as we engage in formal ritual, everyday conversation, and even thoughtful introspection. These thinkers suggest a world without intrinsic properties, in which a reality emerges through what we "do" as social actors, through language. Language does not represent reality, but operates as a mode through which we interpret and engage our worlds. We can apply these frameworks to numbers as symbolic codes as well.[5]

Let's begin with the assumption that our worlds have no intrinsic properties, meaning no objective reality beyond our collective interpretations. This does not imply that human experience is chaotic. Instead, characteristics of elements in our lives come to have meaning through shared human language. Objects do not exist apart from our symbolic interpretation of them. Shared language emerges as the key to an interpretation of meaning. Like verbal codes, numerical codes function in a system of rules and practices, articulated and understood in social communities. If our language and thought do not reflect an external world, then a single, correct description of the world does not exist. As such, there can be no universal claims to reason in everyday life, nor, by extension, in research. Through communication, we seek to reach mutual understandings of what we observe and experience.

How does this argument apply to numerical values? If all properties in our world have no **intrinsic value**, then numbers, in and of themselves, have no intrinsic value. This means that the number seventeen has no meaning in isolation. To understand the number seventeen, we place this symbol between other numbers first, to understand its relational meaning. Seventeen is less than twenty, and much more than four. However, is the number seventeen that different from the number four, when imagining a range of numbers between one and five hundred? The contextual understanding of the numerical value begins with an understanding of the relational nature of this number. This interpretation may seem like an ordinary activity for those of us who tend to think about numbers quite often, but it is an act of interpretation nonetheless.

Once the numerical relation is understood, we attempt to interpret the contextual meaning of that number. This process involves ascribing meaning to a value, which is a necessary step in much of ordinary life, as well as in research. Seventeen dollars for a pair of shoes has a different meaning than seventeen dollars for an ice-cream sundae. Renting a home for $750 a month has a different meaning when shared across several people than when paid by one person. While the numerical value remains the same in each of these cases, its functional meaning is contingent upon an interpretation of its context.

Assuming that symbols have no objective properties, they become understood through social interaction. It is at this stage that some scholars might argue that the only appropriate methodological approach might be ethnographic qualitative research. Alternatively, we need not necessarily move to a completely subjectivist, or situated individual stance, or believe that ethnographic research is the only credible and worthwhile mode of scholarly investigation.

To study social phenomena in a world without intrinsic values may entail observation through numerical descriptions; these descriptors function as a language used by a group of observers sharing a set of rules and expectations. The question is not whether there is merit in using numbers, but how methodological conventions about using numbers might be understood and used by a scholarly community.

We may think about a numerical language as we might about verbal language. Through socialization we learn to interpret each of these sets of codes. Numbers, like words, are symbols. We learn to spell words; we learn to describe numerically coded variables. We learn the rules of syntax and grammar; we learn appropriate uses of different analytical techniques. Disputes over the relative appropriateness of different statistics may be analogous to differences over spelling, syntax, and accents across cultures using the English language.

The Political Context of Research

Research operates as a language, with a vocabulary of concepts, used according to particular rules established through professional communities. Numbers, as one manifestation of a research process, are constructed, just as we are taught how to use verbal and visual codes. In other words, numbers come to have meaning through interpretations of communities. The process of creating numbers also rests on the decisions made by a community of scholars. Through the research process, our subjective experience finds credence when shared with others through established procedures of observation, toward an inter-subjective understanding. It is this process of interpretation of shared experiences and the assumptions surrounding this creative endeavor that need to be recognized and explored.

Research communities act to produce and to legitimate knowledge. The research practices sanctioned by research communities define parameters of appropriate approaches to investigation and interpretation. Whether we assign a relieved or concerned interpretation to a perceived correlation between extent of television viewing and aggressive behavior depends, in part, on our allegiance to a theoretical or political position. For example, the same study demonstrating a correlation between children's exposure to television and intention to act violently may be interpreted as statistically weak, in order to make the political case that television need not be considered a threat, or as statistically present (see Chapter 7), establishing the need for more direct supervision of children's television viewing.

Although philosophers of methodology may differ in their assessment of the unique characteristics of a scientific approach, they tend to agree on the social nature of the process.[6] The basic foundation of this normative approach to empirical investigation builds from the practices and beliefs of scholars within communities. Methodological decisions and interpretations are not independent, but constructed through the shared work and debate of scholars. Seeing research as a product of a social context opens up possibilities for alternative visions of methodological approaches. This social context needs to be further understood as part of a political process. This political construction engages a negotiation across actors advocating particular positions using numbers as strategic tools.

The process of determining appropriate methods and interpreting numbers may be social in nature, in that collective agreement transcends individual argument; however, at another level this process must also be recognized as political. Coding the process as "scientific" lends legitimacy to this as a process of knowing, but avoids recognition of the many decisions that contribute to the shaping and use of numbers.

Seeing an empirical process as socially constructed does not mean that we should deny the political nature of the research context. Although one way of thinking about research as a game implies an assumption that participants are active and equal players, we should also acknowledge the inequality of participants in their ability to shape the rules, or the very structure, of the game. Games involve not only players, but also coaches, owners, and boards of directors, with more capacity than the players to change rules. Similarly, research games are dominated by agencies and groups with the capacity to approve, fund, and distribute research.

Proposing, implementing, and sharing research involve relations of power, between and among donors, researchers, and research subjects. Decisions regarding appropriate subjects, interpretations, and methods may serve different interests.[7] Beyond a pragmatic concern with learning the rules of a scholarship game, it is also important to understand how numbers serve particular interests within a political context.

Research Illustrations

In the context of a "modern" society, the process of enumeration facilitates governments in their allocating resources, assessing taxes and debts, distributing services, and determining political districts. The prominence of numeracy as a political language can be attributed to the work of government bureaucracies, along with the needs of market capitalism and the rules of formal education; in addition to these more hierarchical impositions of literacy, Emigh illustrates how the daily practices of rural Tuscans, in keeping records of debts, rents, dowries, and other social obligations, contributed toward a grounded numerical capacity.[8]

Given the rhetorical power of statistics as commanding a particular authority within the modern nation-state, the enumeration process can become a contested site. Urla demonstrates how Basque nationalist language organizations used survey and census data to assert political leverage within Spain, arguing to preserve their language and cultural identity.[9] Similarly, advocacy groups within the United States have argued over the classification of ethnicities, in the interests of asserting visibility and allocating resources. The material and symbolic value of census statistics articulate a source of power in these debates, beginning with U.S. Congressional hearings in 1975, when La Raza joined other organizations in their argument for collecting data on Spanish speakers, thus contributing to the evolution of an "Hispanic" category. Robbin chronicles the continuation of these debates in the 1990s, when federal agencies negotiated the interests of groups representing American Indian, Hispanic, and African American interests, opposing the inclusion of a multiracial category on the grounds that this might dissipate the coherent visibility of their constituencies, against other groups representing German Americans, Asian Americans, Arab Americans, and others arguing for an expanded list of choices.[10]

While the United States has been negotiating how to create categories to represent ethnic constituencies, the debate within France has been whether to include these categories at all.[11] Those who hope to change the census want the French government to collect data on the ethnic composition of its citizens to illuminate racism and discrimination; those defending an official prohibition on collecting official data on race and religion advocate a secular state based on equality, in which no group is designated for special treatment. Each side justifies its position based on a political stance, the former concerned with the problem of inequality and the latter with the preservation of equality.

Debates over census data offer a particularly useful illustration of the complex character of statistics, meant to contribute to the functioning of the state as well as to allow groups to document their presence and assert their needs. Based on these data, a great number of policy decisions are made, such as the construction of political jurisdictions and the allocation of public resources. Colonial and national histories chronicle how census figures have been used as a form of social control, both in the production of certain categories that constitute institutionally defined knowledge and in the use of these numbers to legitimate policy decisions.[12] Documenting people, their movements, illnesses, and other conditions, serves to facilitate control by governmental and other agencies. Enumeration becomes part of the planning process not only of states, but also of development and other agencies attempting to allocate social services to vulnerable groups. Yet these are the communities often most difficult to count, given the transient conditions of refugees, street homeless, and other marginalized groups.[13]

Another illustration of the political implications of research calls into question the ordinal character of nominal data. Nominal data refer to the categories of measurement for which there is no explicit hierarchical order (such as male/female), while ordinal measures infer some commonly understood order across categories (such as never, sometimes, often, always; see Chapter 5 for more discussion). However, in survey and other research, these nominal-level categories tend to be ordered within a hierarchy of power. For example, surveys prioritize male within categories of gender. Other examples privilege Christian or Protestant under Religion; Caucasian/White under Race/Ethnicity; Married under Marital Status; and Republican under Political Party Affiliation.[14] Although the underlying assumption of nominal data would be that categories have no particular hierarchy, clearly the **research community** establishing the measures works within a political context. Though a subtle process, research reinforces the political structures placing groups in escalating hierarchical steps in our society.

While numbers may be used to support a dominant elite, there is also the potential for numbers to be used in efforts toward resistance. For example, a census coordinated by Palestinian administrators demonstrates an attempt to subvert dominant categorizations of who counts as "Palestinian." Previous institutional enumerations, for example, counted Palestinian constituents within other categories, such as Arab Israelis, whereas the subsequent indigenous exercise administered through Palestinian agencies attempted to include Palestinians living in Jerusalem into the broader community of those in the West Bank and Gaza.[15]

Numbers themselves are not neutral, nor are their representations. Organizations, representing various interests, construct numbers through research, which then justifies policies and legitimizes certain perspectives. One central concern with numbers in research, then, is who has access to the production, distribution, and interpretation of this knowledge. Controversy over how to approximate mortality in Iraq illustrates key differences across political agendas, from governments attempting to minimize the violent consequences of military intervention to advocacy groups hoping to highlight the inflicted damage.[16] The research game may be played by a social community of scholars in a world without intrinsic properties, but this game is situated within a broader structure of political and economic interests. Learning the research game is critical in order to use numbers to question dominant political arguments.

Numerical Literacy

Promoting critical thinking requires numerical literacy. On one level, numerical literacy can be understood as a set of competencies learned in order to comprehend the construction of numerical data. But on a much more fundamental level, numerical literacy engages active critique. Numerical literacy is a form of power, through an ability to interpret and question research. Part of political engagement involves an understanding of the politics of research, particularly as used to justify policies, to allocate resources, and to legitimize identities.

It is not enough just to gain expertise in how numbers are used in the research process: this literacy needs to advance us toward asking the fundamental questions that resist obedient acceptance of numbers as objective truth.

Key Terms

Deductive Process
Inductive Process
Instrumental Value
Inter-subjectivity
Intrinsic Value

Numerical Literacy
Objectivity
Research Community
Subjectivity
Symbolic Value

Reflection Questions

1. If numbers do not represent truth, then why should we use them?
2. Which groups in your society have numerical literacy? How are groups without numerical literacy disadvantaged?
3. What numerical estimates should be under the control of government authorities? Mortality? Income? Marriage?
4. Should the national census gather information on ethnic identity? If so, how?

Exercises

1. Find public opinion research on an issue relevant to current public debate. Discuss how public policy might respond to or resist public opinion.
2. Locate a salary calculator through a Web-based search. Compare a salary figure in your home area to those that would serve as an equivalent in terms of cost of living in other areas.

Notes

1. Refer to http://www.pollingreport.com/iraq.htm to review a collection of U.S. public opinion results on this issue in 2006 as well as http://www.worldpublicopinion.org/pipa/articles/breuropera/74. php?lb=breu&pnt=74&nid=&id for results on other coalition countries in 2005. Public opinion polls in Iraq during 2006 are reported in http://www.worldpublicopinion.org/pipa/articles/brmiddleeastnafricara/250. php?nid=&id=&pnt=250.
2. Methodological constraints are described in http://www.nationalhomeless.org.
3. These estimates are reported by Allied Media (2006); Arab American Institute (2005); Brittingham & de la Cruz (2005); and Salaita (2005).
4. See, for example, Jordan (1992) in her discussion of how home and family contexts guide rituals of television viewing.
5. This framework builds on the work of Wittgenstein (1958) and Rorty (1993).
6. For more discussion of these issues, consider Kuhn (1970), Campbell (1988), and Popper (1959).
7. See Said (1978).
8. See Emigh (2002).
9. See Urla (1993).
10. See Robbin (1993), p. 433.

11. See Chrisafis (2009).

12. See Appadurai (1996); Mitchell (1991); and Zuberi (2001).

13. See Crisp (2003) on the issue of refugees and Farrell & Reissing (2004) on the issue of street homeless.

14. Gallup does rotate "Republican" and "Democrat" in its questions as the first-listed answer (http://brain.gallup.com/documents/questionnaire. aspx?study=P0512059, accessed 4/26/06). However, the other questionnaires reviewed consistently listed first these categories: Male, White, Protestant, Married (Chicago Council on Foreign Relations [2002]; National Organization for Research at the University of Chicago [2003]; Pew Research Center for the People and the Press [2005]; U.S. Census [2000]).

15. See Wilkins (2004).

16. See "Updated Iraq Survey Affirms Earlier Mortality Estimates," October 11, 2006, http://www.jhsph.edu/publichealthnews/press_release/2006/ burnham_iraq_2006.html.

CHAPTER 2

Why Do Research? Questioning the Research Context

W hy do we do research? Research helps us to answer questions, representing as-yet-unresolved mysteries. Through the research process, some of these puzzles may be solved, while new ones may arise. But are the research questions worth asking? Before attempting to solve the mystery through heroic adventure, there must be a good reason to do so. The context of the research, establishing the central cast of characters, along with their motivations, must be understood in order to assess the utility of the research. Why did researchers bother to do this work? Who gets to decide which mysteries are worth solving? Does their justification make sense?

Research helps us answer questions, responding to particular interests. The purpose of the research concerns the motivation of the researchers given institutional parameters, as well as the nature of the research questions explored. First, the purpose needs to be positioned within the sources of the research funding and expertise. Moreover, the institutions and individuals granting permission for this research should be established as part of this research context. Next, the purpose can be identified. The **justification** should establish the originality of the research, documenting other studies of similar subjects to show how the project contributes in ways other projects have not; but even beyond the notion that the research question has not been studied before, researchers should justify the importance of their work. Many research questions have not been studied, but not all need to be. Subsequent assessments of the research process and product are contingent upon the context in which the research has been justified, supported, and implemented.

Who Produced the Research?

Understanding the research game begins with an identification of the institutions supporting the research through funding and hiring researchers, as well as through granting permission for the research. These institutions represent the structure of owners and managers with the decision-making power to determine the rules of the game. While not all of these institutions hold similar power, they offer the financial, expert, and social capital needed for the research to occur.

Researchers' Home Institutions

First, what type of organizations are the identified authors affiliated with? These might be academic institutions, nonprofit research firms, government institutions, corporations, or others. The institutional affiliation of the authors tells us a bit about the potential motivations of the identified researchers. There may also be several different types of organizations represented if there is more than one author on the project. But it is not just the authors who matter: the funding source needs to be recognized as well.

Funding Institutions

Noting the funding institutions is crucial toward understanding the underlying motivations for the research. These funding sources may be explained within the body of the research presentation, or in a footnote or acknowledgement section. Funding institutions may be universities or other academic or professional organizations, public agencies, private firms, philanthropies, or others.

When funding agents are not identified, we should raise concerns with the legitimacy of the research published. For example, when commercial pharmaceutical companies covertly fund experts or medical journals, the value of these scholarly publications is seriously challenged.[1] Similarly, when partisan political parties fund push polls without identifying themselves as sponsors, the credibility of the results is compromised. To illustrate, a Bush campaign in South Carolina asked potential voters: "John McCain calls the campaign finance system corrupt, but as chairman of the Senate Commerce Committee, he raises money and travels on the private jets of corporations with legislative proposals before his committee. In view of this, are you much more likely to vote for him, somewhat more likely to vote for him, somewhat more likely to vote against him or much more likely to vote against him?" The American Association for Public Opinion Research and other public polling organizations critique push polls such as these for disguising themselves as independent surveys rather than acknowledging their funding sources.

Understanding the types of organizations contributing funding to the research helps identify the potential political, theoretical, and economic incentives guiding the research project. Public agencies may be accountable to politicians and political constituencies, in terms of the direction of funding and an assessment of programs. Private funding might be accountable to a variety of stakeholders, such as boards of directors and shareholders, depending on whether the particular institution is geared toward commercial profit or nonprofit gain. While the central motivation of privately run commercial organizations can be more clearly seen in terms of economic profit, nonprofit, nongovernmental organizations themselves can be quite varied, integrating funding from a variety of public, private, commercial, and perhaps even covert agencies. The listing of organizations directly involved in the funding and implementation of research should be included in public presentations, but further investigation of these organizations and their own sources of funding might also tell us more about the motivations for the research project.

Permission-Granting Institutions IRBs, etc.

Once the financial resources provide the researchers with the opportunity to conduct the research, other types of institutions may be called upon to offer legitimacy to the research process. Most universities and state agencies establish research review boards to assess research plans that would involve work with human or animal subjects, particularly important given the current potential and historically enacted unethical treatment of living creatures. Given that the ultimate goal of research should be to help social causes, the process of research should not harm its subject in any way. These institutional review procedures help establish legitimacy for the research process.

Other organizations may also be called upon to grant permission for the research, associated with the research subjects. For example, studies of students would solicit permission from their schools, of employees from their organization, or of members from their club authorities. If this permission is not explicitly acknowledged, then we might question how the researchers gained access to their subjects, and whether the process seemed covert or deceitful. How researchers gain access to their research subjects, using a variety of approaches ranging from complete deception to fully informed consent, is addressed more extensively in Chapter 6.

Before the research is implemented, a community of professionals with expertise in research issues needs to determine how best to advocate for and protect research participants. Embedding this institutional review into the formal process of research is an attempt to address a power imbalance between those conducting (the researchers) and those informing (the subjects) the research. The agency responsible for advocating on behalf of research participants adds another player to the research game, with the responsibility to determine the degree for potential harm against the potential contributions of the study (see Chapter 5), given the particular circumstances and perceived vulnerability of the target group (see Chapter 4). The underlying goal is to create a structure in which an agency advocates on behalf of research participants, who have less power than those conducting the research.

This set of decisions is itself indicative of a political tension, one between those intensely advocating on behalf of the rights of research participants and those intently pursuing a scientific claim. Those in the latter camp are keenly aware of the need in social science to secure a high response rate to lend credibility to their findings (see discussion of sampling issues in Chapter 4). Researchers' interest in having as many as people as possible agree to participate in their data collection corresponds to their political interest in achieving results that can be published and distributed among peers. The pressure of the peer professional group, then, may be at odds with the arguments of others more concerned with the protection of human subjects.

Research legitimacy may be established through these formal procedures, but also through informal mechanisms, articulated explicitly in voluntary practices suggested within professional communities as well as understood implicitly in the norms of cultural contexts. Some codes exist among global actors, such as the World Medical

Association in establishing guidelines on clinical research out of historical concern with the deaths and torture of prisoners subjected to research in Nazi Germany. Professional groups, such as the American Sociological Association, have created codes of ethics to guide professional behavior. These guidelines are not mandatory, not even being enforceable, but establish the parameters of acceptable research practices. Similarly, the American Medical Association and other professional medical groups have advocated guidelines that call for a refusal to accept funding or gift incentives from the pharmaceutical industry, to avoid the actual or even appearance of commercial influence on medical practice.[2] In addition to these stated codes, unstated understandings of what is considered acceptable also influence researchers' decisions.

Decisions about what is ethical and what is not differ not only across cultural context, but also over time. Ensuring the human rights of research participants can be seen as part of protecting civil liberties, which itself is historically and culturally contingent. The infamous experiment chronicling the trajectory of untreated syphilis in 400 poor African-American men in the rural South would not be granted institutional approval in a North American context today. While the historical period matters, so do cultural norms. For example, the issue of informed consent, prominent in the ethical debates in Anglo-Saxon countries, is given far less importance in France, where a patriarchal approach and an emphasis on therapeutic benefit are more prominent.[3]

These differences in cultural norms also translate into varying ways institutions are designed to respond to reviewing research proposals. While the United States relies on an **institutional review board** approach, administered through each institution, other countries, such as Australia, are governed through more centralized research ethics committees, which are responsible to government or quasi-governmental authorities. These institutional review processes can differ substantially, then, in terms of the timing and nature of monitoring as well as which group has the authority to enforce decisions.

What Is the Purpose of the Research?

Given the institutional structure of the research project, the broad purpose of the research can be identified. The purpose might be academic, following a scholarly investigation; evaluative, assessing the performance of a project; or commercial, positioning information as a tool toward achieving profit. These purposes can be motivated by economic interests (as in commercial research) as well as political (in policy and evaluation research) and theoretical concerns (in academic research). These motivations might be rooted in intentions to use research to build knowledge for the purpose of control or emancipation, a tool to facilitate domination or support resistance.

Research may also be fulfilling more than one purpose at a time, contributing to economic, political, social, and academic functions. First, is there a commercial component to the research, funded by a private or corporate entity standing to profit from the accumulated information? Second, is there a political agency or policy group driving the research in order to inform decisions on public issues? Third, might a particular cultural group, social movement, or organization benefit from the knowledge gained through the research? Finally, would the results contribute to academic discussions on a topic?

Evaluation research offers one illustration of how research can contribute to a range of goals, from administrative functions to critical learning. Evaluation of social programs might begin with monitoring of implementation, counting how many staff and program participants appear during events. Moving from management functions to critical assessment, evaluation might assess the immediate outcomes of programs, such as whether program participants learned anything or changed their actions, or attempt to document more long-range consequences, such as policy changes in relevant areas. Evaluations can be narrowly confined to a specific program, or more broadly conceived across several programs or in relation to comprehensive social patterns.

For example, sound research has been conducted evaluating the effects of HIV communication campaigns, contributing to scholarship on media effects. This research might also have the potential to strengthen the work of advocacy organizations (addressing a social purpose) or to inform the decisions of policy makers (contributing to a political purpose). If corporate manufacturers of condoms are included, then this research might also contribute to economic decisions about how to market and distribute their products. Knowing the context of the research project helps explain the potential relevance and utility of the research question and approach.

What Are the Research Questions?

Knowing the sources and purpose of the research project helps in understanding the potential value of **research questions.** The research question guides the project as a whole and should be justified adequately not only in terms of a contribution to knowledge, but also in terms of social relevance. Authors should provide enough discussion of other studies to position their research project as both building on what others have done and adding knowledge not previously documented. This discussion should include what we already know, in relation to what we do not know and still need to know. The authors should explain why their project is relevant given identified social needs.

These questions might suggest an approach that attempts to *describe, explore,* or *explain a* particular social condition. For example, **descriptive research** might chart voting patterns. **Exploratory research** might engage in in-depth study of newly registered voters. **Explanatory research** might contrast the demographics of more recent registrants with those who have been voting consistently since they were eligible to do so. Each of these approaches implies a different set of potential research designs, described in Chapter 3.

Research questions may address broad themes, deductively explained then in more intermediary and specific terms. The broadly defined questions should be apparent within the title of the project and the introductory paragraph, whereas the more specific questions correspond more closely with the research design and approach, which is explained in the methodological section of the research. A well-articulated research project may also pose intermediate-level questions, bridging the broadly identified themes with the more specific issues addressed through data collection. Determining these questions will help guide the potential utility of subsequent assessments of research design and sampling, as well as conceptualization and operationalization.

How Is the Research Justified?

The research questions, building from the **research purpose,** need to be justified on two levels. First, the questions should indeed constitute a mystery that has not yet been solved. A review of other studies that have been conducted on similar topics should help establish what we know and do not know, given the accumulated scholarship on related topics.

But more importantly, are these questions worth answering? There are many things we do not know, but not all deserve the considerable financial and opportunity costs that research requires. Without an ecological concern in mind, it may be pointless to count grains of sand on a beach; similarly, without an application in mind, why conduct a national survey of people's color preferences? Whether the research addresses topics worth considering will require a judgment call from the reader but may be facilitated by the explanations offered as the researchers justify their work.

Why the Research Context Matters

Disputes over numerical estimates pervade public discussion and can often be connected with the institutional agendas of those producing these counts. In estimating the numbers of participants in a political rally, for example, estimates can be offered by the sponsoring organization, as well as police accounts, or remote imaging through other organizational auspices. For example, the National Park Service estimate of 400,000 people participating in the Million Man March in 1995 was critiqued for being too low, inspiring a subsequent study commissioned by ABC that shifted this estimate to 675,000 to 1.1 million.[4] The projected numbers serve as a tool for potential legitimization or marginalization.

Another illustration of the importance of an institutional agenda centers on mortality estimates. In another example, the Johns Hopkins School of Public Health estimated that over 650,000 deaths occurred in Iraq between March 2003 and July 2006, most attributed to violence; this estimate was more than 20 times the number of deaths acknowledged by U.S. President Bush in a speech in December 2005. While the U.S. government would hope to minimize the projection of negative consequences given military intervention in Iraq, the public health school made a strong argument that an international group independent from government agencies should assess the mortality and health conditions of people in areas with substantial violence and conflict.

The insertion of corporate and capitalist interests can also contribute to the structure of research in ways that support these institutional agendas. In a survey sponsored by TV Watch, most registered voters respond that they prefer choosing their own television programming rather than support their government going "too far in its attempt to control what's on television."[5] TV Watch encompasses member organizations such as the American Conservative Union, the U.S. Chamber of Commerce, NBC Universal, and CBS Corporation, which all have a vested interest in limiting governmental intervention in television programming. In addition, the prioritization of profit is all too evident in the case of corporations Syngenta and Ecorisk attempting to influence Professor Hayes' scientific research on the harmful effects of their product, the herbicide atrazine.[6]

Before we can assess the strength of research, we need to have a sense of the research context, recognizing the institutional affiliations of those who have offered financial, expert, and social support for its implementation. The research questions, guided by the purpose of the project, are grounded in the motivations of these agencies.

Key Terms

Descriptive Research
Evaluation Research
Explanatory Research
Exploratory Research
Institutional Review Board

Research Funding
Research Justification
Research Institutions
Research Purpose
Research Questions

Review Questions

1. Who produced the research?
2. Who paid for the research?
3. Who approved the research?
4. What is the purpose of the research?
5. What are the research questions?
6. How is the research justified?

Reflection Questions

1. Who has the power in our society to determine research agendas?
2. How does the purpose of academic research differ from that of commercial research?
3. What kinds of social programs should be evaluated?
4. How can funding institutions influence the research process?

Exercise

Find different estimates of the same phenomenon. For each estimate, determine who conducted and paid for the research. Consider how these research contexts contributed to the production of each numerical estimate.

Notes

1. See Gandy (2010), as well as sources on controversy over Elsevier financial support for medical journals.
2. See Sternberg (2009).
3. See Maio (2002).
4. See Taylor & Lincoln (1997).
5. See AP (2006b).
6. See Blumenstyck (2003).

CHAPTER 3

What Can We Know?
Questioning Research Design

I n this chapter I review the questions we might ask about the **research design** given the parameters articulated in the research context and approach. These questions lead toward exploring what we can know, given a particular research design. The possibilities of what we can understand are limited by the type of comparative opportunities established in the choice of research design. Critiques of research design rarely inspire researchers to cease their projects; rather, these points guide scholars' decisions regarding their design options and their potential interpretations of results. In critiquing research designs, we can suggest alternative structures of comparison that might offer stronger or more relevant accounts.

What Is the Research Design?

First, we should consider the structure of the research process. Based on the type of research approach (addressed in Chapter 2) used, we begin by determining whether the research is exploring one particular case (exploratory research), describing a set of conditions (descriptive research), or explaining a particular condition (explanatory research).

In the first two conditions, a social phenomenon is being explored or described, but no comparison is implied in order to explain a condition or event. For example, a case study of communication patterns among pool players explores this situation in depth. Similarly, a textual analysis of a film does not engage comparisons, but explores particular elements, such as narrative structure or characterizations. The construction of ethnicity in the representation of villains in action-adventure film, for instance, might engage an in-depth study.

With explanatory research, there is a comparative element, toward the purpose of explaining a particular condition. This comparison might be implemented through an experimental design, in which participants are randomly assigned to intervention and control conditions (see Chapter 4 on sampling). For example, one group might see an action-adventure film and another no film, in order to compare the potential effect of the film on attitudes toward terrorism. As long as the individuals are randomly assigned to these groups, the design may be referred to as experimental.

Most social research, though, does not follow these experimental conditions. Research comparing groups that are not randomly assigned into particular conditions is referred to as "quasi-experimental." Quasi-experimental research may compare groups at one particular time, using a cross-sectional design, or over time, using a longitudinal design. In cross-sectional research, comparisons are made across groups who watch television contrasted with people who do not; or texts, such as newspaper coverage compared with television news coverage. In quasi-experimental research, these groups are divided in terms of their own everyday decisions and actions, such as choosing to watch television or read the newspaper. In contrast, in an experimental study the researcher randomly assigns individuals to watch or not watch a television program; participants do not themselves choose whether to watch the program.

With longitudinal research, the comparison, articulated in the research question, occurs over time. With a trend study, for example, surveys of public opinion polls might be contrasted over each year of a particular leader. Or, we might observe prime-time television programs over time to see if female characters' occupations have changed. Cohort studies mark a different kind of longitudinal research, in which one particular group is followed over time. For example, we might have surveyed so-called slackers when they graduated from high school, and then continue to sample this age group as they mature to see if their employment status or political attitudes have changed over time. With a cohort study, the researcher selects a different sample within the same defined group at each point in time. Another longitudinal design engages a panel study, in which the same participants are interviewed each time. We might observe and interview specific slackers over time to chronicle particular events and conditions that contribute to shifts in their opinions and leisure activities.

Once the particular design has been identified, we can follow a set of questions concerning what else might explain the results. Given the logic of each design, particular sets of questions follow.

What Are the Internal Validity Concerns?

The issues raised here pertain to the **internal validity** of the research design. The concept of validity, when applied to research design, serves more as a way of asking questions than as a stamp of approval. Every research design has its strengths and weaknesses and should be assessed in relation to its ability to answer a given research question in comparison with other potential strategies.

First, I review questions we might ask of experimental research designs, when subjects are randomly assigned into the different groups under investigation. Next, I consider **quasi-experimental designs**, in which researchers make comparisons across non-equivalent groups in more natural conditions, observing data over time (in longitudinal models) or across groups at one point in time (in cross-sectional studies). Some research models may elect to combine approaches, comparing groups of people or texts within and across historical moments. Next, I briefly consider the internal validity issues associated with a single case study approach.

Experimental Design

To qualify as an experimental design, groups must be randomly assigned into the categories of investigation (see Chapter 4 for more extensive description of probability sampling strategies). These groups may be referred to as intervention and **control groups**; the former receives the treatment being studied and the latter does not. For example, an intervention group may complete a questionnaire after viewing a television program, while a control group may answer the same questionnaire without viewing that program. Because individuals are randomly assigned into experimental groups, they are assumed to be equivalent in relevant areas other than the particular experimental condition. When comparing across groups that have been randomly assigned, we might assume strong internal validity. If attempting to make a case for media effects, for example, experimental research may be more likely to demonstrate strong correlations than non-experimental designs, as evidenced in a comprehensive meta-analysis across research studies of the effects of pornography use.[1]

If, however, the same group of people is observed before and after experimental conditions, the longitudinal contrast may become subject to internal validity concerns. This critique refers specifically to the component of the design in which one group, as a panel, receives the same test more than once, perhaps before and after viewing a film. While comparisons across randomly selected groups may be assumed to have internal validity, comparisons within the same group over time may be subject to validity concerns, such as research subjects guessing and then responding to researchers' intentions. This issue is addressed in the next section, which reviews longitudinal panel designs.

There are issues other than internal validity to consider with this model. First, experimental models tend to have strong internal validity but lack external validity (reviewed in Chapter 4); in essence, given the artificial nature of the experimental conditions, we cannot assume that responses would be similar in more natural circumstances. Also, at times it may not be feasible to assign people randomly into certain conditions, particularly when we are interested in shifts in historical conditions or in contrasting naturally occurring conditions. There are also instances in which random assignment may not be desirable or ethical, particularly if withholding the intervention or treatment has the potential to harm research subjects. The potential for harm would be balanced against the potential for gain, in understanding how and whether certain interventions, such as medical treatments, might work, before applying them uniformly.

Quasi-experimental Cross-sectional Design

A frequently employed quasi-experimental model uses a cross-sectional approach, comparing groups of observations at one point in time. For example, comparing the attitudes and knowledge of heavy television viewers with light television viewers employs a cross-sectional approach, as would a contrast between women's and men's enjoyment of particular genres of film. Conducted at one point in time, studies of this nature are vulnerable to unique contextual influences present during that historical moment.

articulated independent variables

When groups of individuals are compared at one point in time, they are expected to differ along the dimension of the articulated independent variable. For example, television viewers (the independent variable in this case) may be more likely to believe it is appropriate to act aggressively in conflict situations than people who do not watch television. With this particular research design model, entailing a quasi-experimental, cross-sectional approach, we should consider potential internal validity problems of **selection** and **contamination.**

The issue of selection refers to some pre-existing difference across sampled groups, irrespective of predicted differences. The potential problem is that if we were to observe differences across groups, they may not be attributable to the intended independent variable. For example, we might observe a connection between amount of television viewing and propensity toward obesity, but it would be misleading to assume a causal relationship (see Chapter 7). People who already lead sedentary lifestyles might be more attracted to television viewing in the first place. Similarly, it may not be that women watch more television than men because of their gender, but rather due to their type of employment and available leisure hours in the home.

Researchers should consider possible alternative explanations for projected results before starting research implementation so that they can incorporate these factors into the instrument design. In the examples above, we might include questions regarding hours of employment outside the home or frequency of exercise. In reviewing published research, it is useful to reflect on possible alternative explanations, and then to determine whether these factors have been included adequately in analyses. Gender, socioeconomic status, and ethnicity refer to basic attributes that are often considered in studies of individuals, but there may be other characteristics, such as political or social orientations, that should be included as well. In reading and critiquing research of this nature, selection is the most important threat to the internal validity of a research design.

Critiques addressing selection issues arise when considering alternative explanations for significant results; concerns over contamination offer one explanation for research that does not produce significant results (what is considered significant is addressed in Chapter 7). The threat of contamination occurs when information spreads from the intervention to the comparison site. With a quasi-experimental design, groups are divided according to some established criteria. This division may not reflect the differences intended by the researchers, such that the groups are not comparable. If a political advertisement is shown on television in one city and not another, researchers might hope to contrast political attitudes and intentions across the two sites. However, if members of the comparison community learn about the political advertisement through other people or through the news, then the two sites are no longer comparable.

Quasi-experimental Longitudinal Design

Longitudinal research compares observations over time. In trend studies, different samples of a general population are compared over time, as in a study of voter preferences between 1965 and 2005. A cohort study more specifically targets a subgroup, examining that same group over time. For example, we might study whether adolescents of the 1960s maintained liberal political attitudes as they aged, or whether female assistant professors became more satisfied with their work conditions as they progressed toward becoming full professors. A panel study involves an even more specific model, studying the same individuals over time, such as how a given 10 students may have fared as they advanced through their years in a university setting.

Longitudinal analyses entail many potential threats to internal validity. If the research model being reviewed involves a comparison of data over time, **history, maturation, testing, attrition,** or **instrumentation** might explain the results rather than the intended difference.

Although researchers examining differences over time typically intend to isolate some key factor in explaining results, there are critical contextual differences across historical moments. Assessing the potential for history as a threat to internal validity means understanding the climates and events within and across the time periods studied. Major events, such as military invasion, political elections, and celebrities announcing HIV infections, contribute to the climate within which people learn, form opinions, and take action.

Another potential threat to validity, particularly when examining a cohort or panel sample, involves maturation, or ongoing change within a group. For example, if a university study were to follow a cohort or panel group of university freshmen through their graduation, offering self-esteem workshops at regularly scheduled intervals, the results may not be necessarily attributable to the effect of the workshops but rather to the natural maturation of the students. Similarly, children's changing responses to television over time may not be a result of an educational exercise, but instead of their advancing intellectual and emotional capacities.

When the same group of individuals is assessed over time, as in a panel study, testing should be considered as another potential threat to validity. This concerns whether people's responses to subsequent surveys are colored by their earlier experiences taking the same survey. It may not be that watching an educational video resulted in a change in behavior or attitude, but that respondents had time to consider their responses and perhaps even to guess the intentions of the researchers. Any change, then, across the two surveys might be attributable to the experience of test taking rather than to the intervention. The capacity for students to improve their testing scores, such as the GRE, through practice attests to the importance of this concern.

Attrition is another concern with a panel study, when individuals drop out of the study over time. Research subjects may move, die, or even just tire of the research process. When this happens, the group being studied later in time is no longer comparable to the earlier group, given the different composition of participants. Excluding data from the participants gone from the earlier point in time would inspire other concerns, given that the kind of people who are able to sustain their participation in research over time are substantively different from the others who have left.

Another concern is with instrumentation: the research instrument may change over time, thus influencing results. Survey questions, if changed, may result in different answers over time. Apart from the fairly obvious problems of comparing answers to differently worded questions is the more subtle difference of changed meanings over time. What we understand to be "terrorism" may change over time, for example. Words such as "wicked" and "sick" change over time among particular communities. Or, a list of films including "Spiderman" or "Star Trek" has a different meaning depending on the most recent version released. This concern should also be raised with interviewing, in that over time people conducting interviews become better at the process, perhaps eliciting different types of responses. As the research instrument himself or herself, the interviewer may affect the informant through different approaches and inflections in how questions are asked.

Case Study Design

Case study research allows for an exploration or description of a set of data within a particular context. For example, a study of people listening to radio coverage of 9/11 might constitute a case study approach. Without comparisons of a cross-sectional or longitudinal nature, case studies are subject to many of the internal validity concerns already raised. For example, we would need to consider the selection bias of research subjects. What about that particular group brought them into the condition being investigated? What conditions led to one particular group listening to radio coverage of this event, for example? Without a comparison, we might not know what led some to listen to radio rather than television, or ignore coverage altogether. We also would not understand how radio might have been used differently over time, from the initial events of 9/11 to discussions weeks later. From the case study information, we might know about that group at that point in time, but we could not infer other kinds of differences. Some research using numbers attempts to build on existing case study designs toward comparisons enabling explanatory research possibilities.

Questioning Research Designs

In questioning research designs, the first step is to identify the model. If a comparison is being made, are the groups randomly assigned into experimental conditions? If not, does the quasi-experimental model engage in cross-sectional or longitudinal comparisons? Once the model is identified, there are a series of questions to consider. For example, with cross-sectional designs, selection biases and potential contamination or diffusion of treatment need to be accounted for, but the specific critique will require that we creatively consider the issue at hand in relation to the literature and the context of the study. With longitudinal studies, internal validity concerns such as maturation, history, testing, attrition, and instrumentation should be assessed.

Given the parameters of the research community, it is generally assumed that the internal validity of the research design may be strongest with experimental conditions and weakest with case studies. However, research designs are complex and should be considered on their own terms. It could be that a strong combination of cross-sectional and longitudinal assessment, comparing groups across space and time (such as those exposed to a communication campaign in one community and those not exposed in another, also assessing both groups over time), might offer a more powerful design than an experimental approach. These combination designs tend to require more resources so are not implemented as frequently, but they do help to establish stronger approaches with fewer internal threats to validity. However, internal research validity is but one of many considerations. External validity, concerning the potential to extrapolate across people, place, and time, also matters. This subject will be covered in the next chapter following a review of sampling strategies.

Why Research Design Matters

To illustrate potential political implications of particular research designs, next I describe research evaluations of communication campaigns. Implicit within each design is a set of research questions that can be addressed, as well as those that must be excluded. Discussed here will be the case study approach, experimental, cross-sectional, and longitudinal designs. The political consequences of these evaluations are described in relation to the specific case of media and fertility campaigns, building on an insightful discussion by Hornik and McAnany[2] on the subject.

The case study approach is often used to assess the implementation of campaigns, as well as monitoring direct and immediate consequences. Monitoring asks researchers to explore the processes of implementation in order to chronicle the conditions that contribute to the eventual success or failure of the campaign. Outcomes may also be assessed through the evaluation of a particular project through case study research.

The questions that can be addressed through this approach tend to be more of an exploratory or descriptive nature, assessing how projects are implemented and how participants engaged the issues addressed through the communication campaign. This approach works well in establishing in-depth data and contextual considerations; without a comparison, however, we cannot gauge how participants might have done otherwise, without the intervention. Thus, questions of a more explanatory nature are avoided.

If the project is working well, then there is no evidence on which to base a strong political case for replication. If strong outcome evidence is needed to justify political decisions, then this approach falls short. However, for projects that are still emerging, at their beginning stages, strong empirical evidence demonstrating a lack of effect could prematurely inhibit future funding. Given that one fundamental political concern for institutional projects is basic survival, through continued approval and funding, stronger research designs may be damaging. Selecting a case study approach then might fulfill a political desire to perpetuate projects that might not be able to demonstrate strong outcomes.

One comparative possibility lending stronger empirical evidence of outcomes than a case study approach would be to compare groups who have received an intervention with those who have not. Some evaluations are able to exploit a random selection of participants within an experimental design, such that groups are directly comparable. Given the strong internal validity of this design, this approach is often mandated in testing of medical procedures and substances. While an experimental design enables strong empirical evidence most accessible to political justifications and decisions, it is not always possible, relevant, or even ethical in evaluations of social projects.

Cross-sectional research within a quasi-experimental approach contrasts groups exposed to a project intervention with those who are not. Evaluations of campaigns contrast people who either explicitly remember a campaign with people who do not, or people who should have been privy to campaign information, either through their extensive media exposure (such as heavy television viewing) or geographical proximity (selected sites), with others. This type of evaluation complements the work of campaigns fitting a social marketing model, in which the objective of projects is to affect individuals' knowledge, attitudes, and behaviors through exposure to the message.

This research design allows us to address questions such as: Are people exposed to the communication campaign more likely to have more knowledge of the issues than people who are not exposed? Are people exposed to the communication campaign more likely to have more receptive attitudes than people who are not exposed? Are people exposed to the communication campaign more likely to enact designated behaviors than people who are not exposed?

Within the parameters of the design itself, the research is limited to the extent that the two groups are believed to be comparable. Selection, as a primary threat to validity within this model, implies that people might be divided into those exposed and not exposed on the basis of prior interest in the issues. Also, with any study relying on correlations of this nature, the issue of causality should be raised. The direction of potential effect is not clear: given observations at one point in time, previously held attitudes and behaviors might as easily make memory of a communication more salient as that message might encourage shifts in knowledge, attitudes, and behavior.

In comparison with a case study approach, a cross-sectional design may allow for stronger comparisons, but then is limited in terms of the in-depth information that would be possible to explore. Hornik and McAnany describe processes potentially relevant to fertility decisions, such as how groups engage in discussions of gender roles, relate media narratives to personal experiences, interpret broader public discourse on pertinent issues, and engage in selection of media programs. In relation to longitudinal approaches, this design is also limited in that one cannot know the degree to which findings represent a particular historical moment, or a long-term historical trend.

Politically, a comparative approach can be useful in offering stronger empirical evidence of effects than other research designs. In comparison with a case study approach, a cross-sectional design offers some basis for demonstrating that those exposed to the campaign are different than others in key outcomes. Longitudinal data, however, might demonstrate that observed changes over time may be part of longer-term trends, and thus not related to the campaign experience at all. If the political need is to justify future funding of a project, this design is closely tied to the implementation of the project. If other political needs are identified, however, such as the long-term conditions of a particular community, then longitudinal observations might be warranted.

Longitudinal research allows the comparison of groups over time. With an evaluation of a campaign, we might observe patterns of knowledge, attitudes, and practice before and after the implementation of the project. This research allows an assessment of whether people exposed to a campaign have increased their knowledge of the selected issues, changed their attitudes, or shifted their behaviors. Other conditions can be assessed over time, such as attendance at health clinics, telephone calls to hotlines, and purchases of condoms.

While this design does allow us to discern change over time, what can be known is first limited to the time period studied. Most evaluations, according to Hornik and McAnany, are conducted in too brief a time period to observe more long-term effects, which would enable us to assess whether the campaign effects themselves are short-lived, or the degree to which the changes are part of ongoing, long-term trends. In their assessment of project evaluations, outcomes may be immediate but not sustained, or assessed too early to discern change. Moreover, without longitudinal data over longer periods of time, it is difficult to assess the extent to which contraception use and attitudes might be part of historical trajectories related to women's educational advancement and changing roles in society.

Similar to the limitations of the cross-sectional approach, this longitudinal approach also may lack an in-depth assessment of the processes through which change occurs. More in-depth analysis of a particular case, for example, might help sort out whether media affect fertility behavior through actual content, or through time spent using media at the expense of other activities.

Against the cross-sectional approach, the longitudinal design lacks comparisons that would enable us to sort out potential effects of history within the context of the society and of maturation of the group of targeted participants. This concern is particularly relevant given Hornik and McAnany's conclusion that the evidence of campaign effects is less strong than that of broader long-term effects.

To observe more sustained effects and to distinguish campaign effects from overall trends, data need to be collected over longer periods of time. However, evaluations are typically tied to funding cycles of donors, which occur in shorter durations. Whereas a donor might want to understand the immediate effects prior to renewing funding for a project, the actual effects may be more discernable over an extended time frame. The political need to justify spending may be inconsistent with the processes engaged by the project.

Key Terms

Attrition	Internal Validity
Case Study Design	Longitudinal Design
Cohort Study	Maturation
Contamination	Panel Study
Control Group	Quasi-experimental Design
Cross-Sectional Design	Research Design
Experimental Design	Selection
History	Testing
Instrumentation	Trend Study

Review Questions

1. What is the research design?
2. What are the internal validity concerns?

Reflection Questions

1. Why are experimental designs not used more frequently?
2. How could research designs using cross-sectional comparisons be strengthened to avoid the problem of selection?
3. What could be the political appeal of panel studies?

Exercise

Find a published research study with enough information to enable you to identify the research design. Then, consider the potential threats to internal validity given the design, and discuss those most relevant to this study. Discuss alternative explanations that might help explain the study's findings.

Notes

1. See Allen et al. (1995).
2. For a comprehensive, insightful analysis of fertility campaigns, see Hornik & McAnany (2001).

CHAPTER 4

Who Is the Research About?
Questioning Selection Strategies

G iven the questions and approach of the study, we can then identify who or what is being studied. The subject of the research may be people, in the form of individuals, couples, groups, organizations, or some other configuration, but it might also be other types of creatures (such as cats or dragons) or social artifacts (such as media texts, graffiti, or museum exhibits). If the subject refers to people, we should determine whether the focus is on individuals, groups, or more formal organizations. Research might study individual journalists, professional associations of editors, or the news organization as a whole. Scholars could also study characteristics of a person (such as aggressive behavior) or interactions (such as conversations). If social artifacts such as media texts become the subject, we might focus on words, visuals, films, characters, genres, or other categories. In considering issues of sampling, we begin by asking what or whom the research is about, and then how the actual selection of people or things studied reflects the intention of the researchers. Moreover, understanding this selection process as an act of power between the researcher and those who are subject to the research raises critical ethical issues. These questions help us to consider how to interpret research findings within the domain of the research itself as well as its relationship to the social and political context in which the research is conducted and used.

The research question or title should help establish the projected subject of the research. How this subject then becomes defined as a particular data source and the procedures through which these sources become selected for the study contribute to the **external validity** of the research.

Who or What Is the Subject of the Research?

The subject of the research should be identifiable in the title of the research project and in the description of the methodological approach. Distinct from the purpose of the research, in this chapter we question whom researchers have actually studied. Building on a broadly defined community of subjects, such as university students, television programs, or fictional characters, researchers need to define the parameters of their pool of **research subjects.** These definitions help us to understand which subjects would get included and which would not. In studying university students, researchers might decide to work within a particular setting and to limit attention to full-time undergraduate students rather than all enrolled. Television programs may need to be defined in terms of channel, genre, scheduling, and inclusion of commercials. Fictional characters might be defined in terms of number of speaking lines. These decisions determine the actual group studied in relation to the **population** that researchers hope to discuss.

Before turning to how subjects are selected for research, it is worth considering the political dynamics between researchers and the researched, particularly in terms of ethical issues raised when working with vulnerable populations.

Vulnerable Populations

While those conducting research have more control over the research events than the subjects of research, this inequality becomes even more pronounced when the populations being studied are vulnerable. Groups might be considered vulnerable when they have relatively less power in the broader political context as well as in the research process, making them even more susceptible to potential exploitation. Some illustrations of vulnerable groups used in research include studies with people involuntarily committed to institutions such as prisons or psychiatric wards, students and children, and those in communities or countries with few material resources or social privileges. In one case, a vulnerable group of intellectually challenged children in U.S. public schools was injected with hepatitis in 1963 in order to study the trajectory of the disease. As a population of convenience, researchers may select vulnerable groups in part due to their low cost and availability, yet their ability to agree to volunteer to participate in research studies is constrained by their individual as well as structural circumstances.

Cheaper cost also explains why researchers in wealthy countries might be tempted to target subjects in less wealthy countries, despite the potential for exploitation. In one illustration, researchers conducted a controversial study of women in South Africa infected with HIV.[1] Following conclusive research in wealthy countries establishing that pregnant women were less likely to pass on HIV infection to their infants when treated with the drug zidovudine, the provision of this drug to infected pregnant women became a matter of standard practice in the United States. However, the cost to do so, at US $800 per woman, was deemed too high for others in developing countries. To test whether a cheaper drug regimen would have similar benefits, researchers informed pregnant infected women in South Africa that they would be randomly assigned to receive a placebo or a cheaper version of the drug. Those in the placebo condition were being denied a treatment that evidence had already demonstrated would be clearly beneficial to the health of their children. Rather than considering other designs that might have offered better care for the women and their families, researchers argued that given local conditions, women were not worse off than they would have been otherwise. The dominant concern was not the well-being of the research subjects, but instead the potential profit of the pharmaceutical industry. Those with power in the broader society, in this case being the commercial firms producing and distributing these medications, were able to dominate decisions about the research process that had serious effects on the health of research subjects.

How Are Subjects Selected?

Understanding the subject of the research is paramount to assessing whether research claims make sense given the intention of the project. Once the subject of the research has been identified, the next set of questions pertains to how these people, groups, or objects have been selected for study. This selection process needs to be understood in relation to the stated objectives of the researchers (see Chapter 2) to establish the potential for external validity. First, the sampling strategy needs to be assessed.

The next set of questions addresses how the particular subjects for the research have been selected. The population refers to the broad group of people or things a researcher wishes to study, the **sample** refers to the actual group studied. At times the population and sample are the same, when the number of elements in a population is of a size that the research group can observe. For example, a population might be defined as all players of a particular video game not widely in circulation, or all political advertisements about a candidate in a designated city. If the sample used for the research then includes all game players or all advertisements identified as members of that population, then we can assume the sample represents the population.

Researchers choose to sample when the elements of a population are too numerous to observe. Sometimes it is just not possible to study each and every person or text, given the human and financial resources available to the researchers. Decisions regarding whether and how to sample also relate directly back to the stated research question, establishing a correspondence between what researchers state they intend to study and what they actually study. When researchers decide to select elements from the population for a sample to study, there are a variety of ways they can do so. In determining the sampling approach, the reviewer should first ascertain whether the researchers used probability or non-probability sampling techniques.

Probability Sampling

The selection process might involve **random** selection procedures, producing probability samples. **Probability samples** involve procedures through which each element has an equal or known chance of being selected. A simple random procedure, such as a lottery, might involve blindly selecting some elements of a known population. There are times, however, when all members of a population are not known. If a researcher uses a telephone book as a method for selecting respondents for a survey, that telephone book would constitute a sampling frame, clearly different from the population in several important respects. To include persons who do not list their telephone numbers, researchers might use a random-digit dialing procedure, creating random numbers for known telephone prefixes, reflecting appropriate proportions.

Other probability sampling techniques might be used for ease and efficiency, such as a **systematic sampling** approach. With this approach, each of the elements of a population are known and listed. A telephone directory or an inventory of top-grossing films would allow us to select names of people or films from known lists, for example.

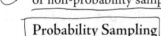

With this procedure, a researcher would select a certain number of names from this list, at established sampling intervals. The sampling interval would first be established by dividing the desired sample number by the known population number. For example, in a list of 100 films, if the desired sample were to be 20, then the interval would be 5. The next step involves selecting a random number between one and that sampling interval number. Sampling can proceed then by selecting every next element established by the sampling interval. If the random number selected were to be three, then the third, eighth, thirteenth, and from there on every fifth element would constitute the final sample of 20 films.

This process may be limited by **periodicity**, or a potential pattern in the listing that would create a sample not typical of the population. If, for example, a researcher wanted to study newspaper coverage of technology, and established a sampling interval of seven in order to select days of the week to observe, then the final sample might include only those papers published on Wednesdays. This might be a real problem if the newspaper devotes Thursdays to a particular focus on technology. This concern would also be relevant to other issues pertaining to days of the week in terms of leisure activities, or houses on a suburban block (if every tenth house is on a corner lot, for example).

A modification of these procedures might involve more complicated processes, through a **stratified** random sampling process. If particular categories of a group exist, we could select randomly within groups at different levels. Within a university setting, for example, we could select colleges, and then departments within colleges. If the sampling frame is known in advance, this would still constitute a probability selection process.

When a population is not known, we can still employ random selection procedures, such as a cluster sampling technique. With these approaches, groups are identified and selections made within each group in a hierarchical fashion. We might randomly select states for a political poll, and then voting districts within these selected states, for example.

Non-probability Sampling

With **non-probability sampling** methods, the chance that you might select any given element in a population is not known. A **convenience sample**, as a classic illustration of this approach, involves selecting participants in terms of ease and availability. A television reporter might stand on a corner and interview people who walk by, for example, or a market researcher might ask shoppers in a mall to complete brief questionnaires. The issue with this approach is that the participants selected for study are not representative of a broader population. Those who happened to be on that corner or in that mall at that time are not similar to the larger communities within which they reside.

Quota sampling builds on this reliance on available participants, but adds a step toward ensuring that the sample represents particular characteristics of a population. A researcher might attempt to study an equivalent number of men and women in a shopping mall. Or, a study of university students might set quotas on the proportion of freshmen, sophomores, juniors, and seniors to participate.

Another non-probability method uses **purposive sampling**, selecting elements based on the purpose of the sample. A study of television producers might use purposive techniques, selecting as many as can be found at a convention. Or, we might study representatives of fraternities and sororities on campus. If the purpose of the study is to observe this population, then that might be an appropriate selection technique for that research question. If, however, we want to generalize to the university community, then selecting these organizations would not create a representative sample.

When no known lists about a particular group exist, then a **snowball sampling** technique might be warranted. With this approach, an initial key informant refers the researcher to others, who then become referents themselves to new informants, thus producing a chain effect. With no sampling frame, this technique helps to build a sample for the research. This is a particularly useful approach toward finding persons engaged in sensitive or controversial activity, such as drug dealers or sex workers.

Focus groups also tend to use non-probability techniques for selecting participants to be interviewed as part of a group by a research facilitator. Focus group informants may be selected purposively by the researcher, or through a key informant. Whether the composition of the group is initiated by the researcher or subject, the process of selection corresponds with these non-probability techniques.

What Are the Limitations of the Sample?

The research process often results in the identified sample not matching the described population. Even in the cases described above, some video game players might refuse to be interviewed, or some advertisements might be lost. The resulting sample then involves some sample bias, meaning that the people or texts constituting the research sample are not typical of the broader population they are meant to reflect. If not stated by the researchers themselves, it is worth considering how the actual pool of research subjects relates to the intended population, in order to establish the sample's limitations.

Some of these limitations establishing a particular bias might result from the type of selection strategy pursued, or from the actual process of attempting to elicit permission for the research. In the first regard, non-probability samples would not represent a broader group, but only the individuals or objects selected for study. In the process of selection, **sampling bias** might occur when people are not accessible for observation or interview, refuse to participate, or have trouble understanding or participating in the study. Sampling bias might occur with texts when organizations grant access to some documents or programs and not others, when archives include some materials but discard others, or when technical difficulties result in the inclusion of some websites and not others. Using these illustrations as a guide, the reviewer should consider what research subjects are included, what is excluded, and how that exclusion limits the sample.

The limitations to the sample can also be understood in terms of the external validity of the research subjects. To address this issue, the reviewer should first recall the stated research questions or intentions (Chapter 2) and then the subject of the research. Limiting what we can know, as a result of our research, to what has actually been observed builds toward this concern with external validity. External validity refers to the relationship between the particular research project and the wider context in which it was conducted. These questions refer to the context of the research, in terms of the subject (people or texts), place, and time. First, we should not generalize beyond the specific subjects studied. If college students constitute the sample of research subjects, then we can say in conclusion that we understand how these college students react, but not the reactions of a broader community of students. If the *New York Times* serves as the subject of study, we cannot infer that we understand all of the U.S. news.

Second, the place in which the research project was conducted is also critical to the research results. We cannot assume that a study of high school students in New Jersey would find similar results among high school students in Texas. Cultural context needs to be recognized as a critical condition within research observations. An important critique arises with respect to the predominance of research conducted in the United States, assumed in publication to transcend cultural or national differences. Research on audience responses to television, for example, finds diverse responses across nations, so it is a mistake to assume that research findings in the United States could be generalized across humanity.

Finally, the particular historical moment of the research matters as well. Research conducted on computer use, for example, would take on very different meanings in this age compared with even 20 years ago. Studies of fear of terrorism are contingent upon timing as well, whether conducted before or after catastrophic events. The point here is that research conducted at a particular time tells us about that point in time; we cannot infer that the results would be similar further in the past or projected into the future.

One might consider the connection between the broad focus of the study, articulated in the purpose or question of the research, and the specific group actually observed. For example, in an introduction to a research project, authors might state that their goal is to understand the connection between viewing sexual content on television and subsequent attitudes toward sexuality in our society. We might read on further to discern that the researchers have selected college students as their research subjects. The first issue, then, is defining who actually was studied, in relation to what the researchers claim they had hoped to study. Even more problematic might be if this identified purpose was to understand attitudes, yet the sample of the study constituted a set of media texts.

Similarly, researchers might state that their central question concerns how U.S. news frames federal government responses to national disasters, while the particular subject of the research focuses exclusively on the *New York Times*. In each case, findings are limited to what has been observed, as a group of college students or a collection of *New York Times* articles. The act of research necessarily involves the selection of something to observe: the limitation, however, is that resulting interpretations and conclusions need to be confined to the domain of what specifically has been studied.

Why Selection Strategies Matter

Selection strategies matter most when populations of people or artifacts are not accessible to the researcher, due to either the size or the nature of the group. If a population is known, then random sampling techniques might be used to select a useful sample of items. With a population of unknown participants, though, particularly those difficult to identify, such as people dealing illicit substances or living in transitional shelters, attempts to select informants become more difficult. In an attempt to estimate the prevalence of homelessness, some studies use random sampling techniques to select service providers and request information on numbers of people seeking assistance. Other studies have randomly selected people through telephone surveys to assess past experience of homelessness, which again limits the results to those who have telephones and answer them at that time.[2]

Political and economic issues contribute to decisions made in these selection strategies that determine the parameters of the subject pool. "Limited resources" constrained the potential to call back respondents in a telephone survey of Los Angeles County residents more frequently to approach a higher response rate. While the economic support for research can inhibit researchers' potential to pursue stronger selection strategies, political conditions also play a major role. Another telephone survey, this time attempting to approximate Israeli national pride in relation to television exposure, culminated in excluding Arab respondents in analyses because of the sensitive and contentious nature of questioning about loyalty to the Israeli state, given this community's marginality within the broader political structure.[4] A third illustration of a telephone survey also relied on randomly generated numbers but oversampled areas with expected higher concentrations of African-American, Hispanic, and Asian teens, often done when researchers expect to focus on particular groups that might otherwise be less proportionately represented.[5] While the intention of probability sampling techniques is to approximate a broader population, political and economic circumstances may produce samples that differ substantially from the population they are meant to represent.

Key Terms

Convenience Sampling	Quota Sampling
External Validity	Random Sampling
Focus Groups	Research Subject
Non-probability Sampling	Sample
Periodicity	Sample Bias
Population	Snowball Sampling

Probability Sampling   Stratified Sampling
Purposive Sampling   Systematic Sampling

Review Questions

1. Who is the subject of the research?
2. How are subjects selected?
3. What are the limitations of the sample?

Reflection Questions

1. Is it justified to use sampling strategies to assess the quality of national census statistics?
2. What would be the political appeal of a convenience sample?
3. How could presumed periodicity in a neighborhood be used strategically to influence the results of a systematic sampling approach?

Exercise

Find a story of interest in the news that uses convenience sampling to interview members of the public on a given topic. Then locate research on the same topic that uses a probability sampling strategy. Compare the findings highlighted across these accounts.

Notes

1. See Schüklenk (2000).
2. See Busby (2006); Drever (1999); National Coalition for the Homeless (2005); U.S. Department of Housing and Urban Development (2004).
3. See Dixon (2008).
4. See Cohen (2008).
5. See Niederdeppe et al. (2007).

CHAPTER 5

What Is the Research About?
Questioning Key Terms

The research topic can be defined on several levels, from the more broadly conceived subject of the research to the more specifically identified **variables** used in data collection. The broad topics might be identified through the title of the publication or through the introduction, explaining the purpose and justifying the importance of the research. These themes might be further specified in reviews of other studies done on similar topics, as well as descriptions of methodological approaches.

In this chapter, we consider how key terms are **conceptualized** broadly, as well as defined more specifically. Given these definitions, we can then question what we know about these terms, as measured through the process of data collection, assessed through their reliability, validity, and precision. How key terms are defined needs to be positioned within the political contexts of the groups conducting and funding the research.

How Are Key Concepts Defined?

First, the reviewer must identify the central topics of the research. Although these may be clearly stated in research questions, at times we might need to read through more complex discussions to identify the substantive issues being addressed. Once these concepts are identified, then we can explore how they have been defined. These definitions might be clearly and explicitly stated, with citations offering a history of how others have defined concepts in similar or in different ways. When not clearly defined, there may be an expectation that conventional wisdom dictates a perceived common understanding of the term. For example, researchers might study "voting" or "watching television" without explicitly theorizing the history of these terms, given a sense that these terms are generally understood, while concepts such as "cynicism" or "anomie" might be more abstractly rooted. In either case, however, there are many decisions made in defining terms that will help determine research results. Violence could encompass verbal as well as physical threats, or could be limited to physical touching with malicious intent. Watching television might refer to the apparatus being turned on, or be restricted to focused attention on visual and audio images. Clarifying how concepts are explicitly defined or implicitly assumed contributes toward a better assessment of how these key terms are used in research.

These definitions help guide how the researchers gather data. To observe violence, for example, would require clear definitions concerning physical and verbal interactions as well as actual and threatened attempts. Given how many different ways there are to define and measure concepts, these decisions need to be understood in relation to the political argument that the source of the research may be attempting to advocate. Defining concepts such as pornography or violence, for example, becomes contingent in part upon political and moral interests in emphasizing or marginalizing concerns with particular media content.

The more concretely defined concepts that allow for observation are typically referred to as "variables" in most social science research texts. The term "variable" is used to describe an observable and varying condition. Temperature can be observed as it varies from one measurement to another, for example. Setting the parameters of observation, determining what to include or exclude, can be connected to a political context in which groups may be attempting to advocate for a particular cause. Asserting that children's television is violent, for instance, would require some questioning as to how we define children's television, as well as violence.

Decisions made about these operational definitions help to shape the data that are produced in the research process. Violence will be seen as much more prevalent if its definition is more broadly based—for instance, including verbal as well as physical, and threatening as well as actual content. The more inclusive the **operationalization** of the term, the higher the rate of incidence we would be able to document. If a group has an interest in establishing a particular condition, perhaps as a central problem (such as violence) or as a valued achievement (such as nutritional status), then there would be reason to use a more inclusively defined variable.

Noting how specifically questions are asked can also point to some potential perspectives evident in the structure of the research. When a survey asks respondents whether they believe the government should monitor Internet searches of "ordinary Americans," privacy interests are privileged over security concerns.[1] When respondents are asked whether they speak Basque or not, this emphasizes ability; when the questions over time were adapted to ask if they spoke well, with difficulty or not at all, degree competence could be assessed.[2] The very operational definition of "homeless" in general vs. "street homeless" itself has implications for who would be eligible to be counted, as well as which sites would be appropriate for observation or documentation.[3]

Once the variables have been operationalized, other factors in research implementation come into play. Assessing the quality and utility of data builds from understanding how terms are defined. These issues are considered next.

What Do We Know about Key Variables?

In reading research, once the definitions of key terms are understood we can question what is known about each variable in the study. Numerical summaries of variables, depicting the range, distribution, and central tendencies, such as **mean, median,** and **mode** statistics, can be assessed in order to consider the **validity, reliability,** and **precision of measurement**.

Measurement

The data created through peoples' responses (such as to structured questionnaires) or researchers' codes (whether created inductively of open-ended conversations or of social artifacts) become listed in particular ways that create different levels of measurement. When a list of responses or codes has no preordained order and could be rearranged without losing the meaning of the list, then the measurement is considered **nominal**. Nominal-level data might include a list of colleges, television programs, religious affiliations, or political organizations. **Ordinal**-level data assume that there is a conventionally understood hierarchy in this list, such as: never, sometimes, often; or no high school education, high school degree, undergraduate degree, more than an undergraduate degree. **Interval**-level data maintain this basis of order but includes an additional feature of assuming equal spaces between each category, such as years of age or a three-point agree/neutral/disagree scale. The **ratio**-level measurement assumes each of the interval-level characteristics, adding in the idea of a zero that makes sense (this itself being a product of political and philosophical decisions). While age may not be assumed to have a meaningful zero, numbers of hours watching television or years of education may.

As described in the introductory chapter of this book, we can infer a political hierarchy to the ordering of nominal categories. The reviewer should examine the way the variables are measured. These descriptions may be included in a methodology section, appendix, or footnotes, or in the results section. Nominal categories may be in alphabetical order, but when not, the prioritization of some categories within the list may help identify the perspectives of the researchers, whether directly applying or subtly reinforcing dominant biases within their social context. For example, privileging the categories of male, Caucasian, Christian, Republican, American, married, heterosexual, and others may resonate with the hierarchies within a current power structure.

The **level of measurement** also determines what statistics can be used to describe data. Variables might be summarized in terms of a central mode, a median, or a mean. The mode refers to the most frequent response or code. The median refers to the middle response, given the order of possible responses. The mean refers to the average of all responses. Given that there is no appropriate order to a nominal-level variable, the only appropriate statistic would be the mode. Ordinal-level variables might use a mode but could also appropriately include a median as a summary statistic. Only interval- and ratio-level variables can employ a mean, given that an average assumes a particular order as well as equal spaces between categories.

However, just because interval and ratio levels of measurement *can* use means does not imply that this would be the best statistic. This decision would depend on the political argument we would wish to assert. Consider statistical descriptions of income. When there are points of extreme deviation, the mean is affected, making a group with a few wealthy individuals appear more well off than they would seem if the median were used, which would be a better indicator of how the majority in that group fared. Most discussions of income and poverty within official publications in the United States therefore rely on median statistics.[4] But when averages are used to describe central tendencies, it is worth questioning whether there is a political advantage to having the variable weighted toward a few deviant cases.

Assessment

Based on the information provided on the measurement of each variable, we may also be able to assess reliability, **validity**, and precision. The precision of the categories defining a variable can be evaluated given the analytical needs of the research. It might be enough to know whether someone watched television news yesterday or not in some analyses, but other projects might need more precise characterizations—perhaps the number of hours a viewer watched television during that day. While analysis makes it possible to move from more to less precise categorizations through recoding procedures, we cannot work in the inverse direction, adding categories to a list once the data have been collected. It might seem, then, worth measuring variables initially with as much precision as possible. However, given the converse relationship between precision and reliability, including numerous categories may limit the quality of analysis in other ways.

Reliability refers to expected consistency in responses and codes. If a respondent agrees to a statement that she is happy, we would expect a consistent response to be disagreement that she is unhappy. If an informant expresses great enthusiasm for a person one day, a consistent response would be to maintain that enthusiasm a week later. If a researcher codes a color as green during one observation period, she would be expected to code that shade as green again another time. Several public opinion polls have asked respondents in the United States about their attitudes toward military intervention in Iraq. Responses appear to have reliability when similar proportions of respondents oppose intervention, whether the question is asked in an initially supportive way (55 percent opposed when asked by a CBS news poll: "Looking back, do you think the United States did the right thing in taking military action against Iraq, or should the U.S. have stayed out?") or in a challenging tone (53 percent opposed U.S. intervention when a USA Today/Gallup poll asked: "In view of developments since we first sent out our troops to Iraq, do you think the United States made a mistake in sending troops to Iraq, or not?"). However, we could include other U.S. public opinion polls also conducted between February and March 2009 to illustrate that responses are not reliable, when more respondents object when the question is asked clearly and directly (67 percent opposed when a CNN/ Opinion Research Corporation poll asked: "Do you favor or oppose the U.S. war in Iraq?"). Reliability can be assessed through statistical measures, but it also relies on selection and interpretation to make the case for consistency.

Other aspects of measurement might constrain the potential for reliability. As the number of possible categories increases, improving the precision of the measurement, reliability may be reduced. If the possible codes are green and white, then the researcher might more consistently code similar shades as green; if the codes include forest green, teal, sea foam, and aquamarine, then there may be divergence in assessments. Similarly, a person might more consistently describe himself as happy or unhappy, or loving or hating, than consistently selecting the same number on a seven-point scale rating the degree of happiness or love.

The quality of the measure can be considered in terms of its reliability, which is typically assessed through statistical procedures, but also in terms of its validity, which is in part evaluated through statistics but more often through conventional wisdom. The validity of the measure, pertaining to the relationship between the observed data and the object of study, matters to the legitimacy of the research. For example, if someone says: "I love you," you might hope that expression, the observed articulation, actually corresponds with an internal feeling. Ideally, we would want this expression to be both valid (as meaningful) and also reliable (consistently stated). Researchers hope that observed data represent an accurate indication of what they intend to study, in a consistent fashion.

Why Definitions Matter

Being clear about definitions matters if others wish to replicate similar studies in other places with other texts or people. In terms of reliability, clarity in definition would allow other researchers to assess similarities and differences in findings with other research projects. A study of television violence, for example, would require shared definitions of this act in order to compare instances across genre, country, or time period.

Definitions also matter because they can be constructed to advance political arguments. How terms are defined might indicate an allegiance to a particular political position. Defining violence in fairly conservative terms with narrow parameters would perhaps serve an interest in observing fewer situations of violence in the media, whereas a more inclusive definition would support the beliefs of advocates concerned with the presence of violence in media.

How variables are measured determines the nature of possible responses. Exploring the specific questions asked of informants helps us to critique the validity of these measures. When definitions of political participation become operationalized by asking respondents if they have voted in a recent election, this restricts the parameters of political engagement to the formal sphere, rather than opening up space for political protest. The careful distinction made by many researchers between meeting for social as opposed to political purposes similarly narrows attention to attempts to affect government policy, as opposed to considering the political nature of action outside of the policy arena.[5]

In another example, a widely used scale assessing rape myth acceptance has been employed by researchers attempting to predict respondents' attitudes toward sexual violence.[6] Respondents are asked to indicate their level of agreement to statements such as: a woman who goes home with a man on their first date implies that she is willing to have sex; when women go around braless or wearing short skirts and tight tops, they are just asking for trouble; in the majority of rapes, the victim is promiscuous or has a bad reputation.[7] As an illustration of validity issues, we might critique these items as measuring attitudes toward women's sexuality more broadly rather than more specifically toward rape.

Studies replicating attitudinal studies, such as the rape myth acceptance scale, may build on the strength of previous research in establishing reliability and validity in measurement. However, including other questions may make the issues more current and relevant, while adding some open-ended items would allow more inductive analytical methods that would illustrate how informants conceptualize key terms, such as "rape" and "sexual abuse," separate from their legal definitions. The potential to establish prevention and treatment interventions is guided by our ability to understand the conditions contributing to these acts of violence.

Whether a scale with a long history holds currency needs to be assessed in each new context in which it is used. Rosenberg's self-esteem scale (first used in the United States in the 1960s) is one of the most widely used in sociology; it has achieved credibility through repeated tests of reliability and validity across many samples of people in different places and over time. This scale combines similar responses to agreement and disagreement to ten statements: On the whole, I am satisfied with myself; At times, I think I am no good at all; I feel that I have a number of good qualities; I am able to do things as well as most other people; I feel I do not have much to be proud of; I certainly feel useless at times; I feel that I'm a person of worth, at least on an equal plane with others; I wish I could have more respect for myself; All in all, I am inclined to feel that I am a failure; I take a positive attitude toward myself. These individual answers are combined to create a scale meant to reflect researchers' definition of self-esteem.

It is not only the method and source of data collection that matter, but also these very definitions that matter. Homelessness, for example, might need to be defined to determine how sleeping in a transitional shelter or family/friends' housing would count.[8] While USHUD carefully defines "unsheltered homeless" as those residing in places not meant for this purpose, such as cars, parks, and streets, advocacy groups argue that those in emergency and temporary housing should also be included. Counting unsheltered persons helps service providers determine distribution of resources, consider future services needed, and request funds from government agencies and other funding sources.[9] Given the wide variation in approaching this estimation through methodological approaches, from one-quarter of a million to over 3 million,[10] it is not surprising that advocacy groups base their concerns on much higher counts of homelessness than that of official estimates by agencies, who are interested in expending fewer resources and projecting successful intervention.[11]

Key Terms

Conceptualization	Operationalization
Interval	Ordinal
Mean	Precision
Measurement Validity	Ratio
Median	Reliability
Mode	Variable
Nominal	

Review Questions

1. How are concepts defined?
2. How are variables operationalized?
3. What do we know about key variables?

Reflection Questions

1. What would be the political appeal of using a mean rather than a median to describe housing prices in a neighborhood?
2. How would you measure wealth if you wanted to argue that a group was quite privileged? How could you change that measurement to advocate for this group as disadvantaged?

Exercises

1. Find a close-ended research survey. Locate the variables measured through nominal categories. Consider the hierarchy of categories used. Are they listed in alphabetical order? If not, what else might explain the order in which categories are listed?
2. Select an issue that has been the subject of more than one research project. Compare definitions of a key term across projects. Consider how the results of each project might relate to how that term has been defined.

Notes

1. See AP (2006a).
2. See Urla (1993).
3. See Farrell & Reissing (2004).
4. See, for example, DeNavas-Walt et al. (2005).
5. See review of literature by Cho & McLeod (2007).
6. See Burt (1980).
7. More detailed and additional items serve as part of the larger scale used in research projects; this is described in Allen et al. (1995).
8. See NCH (2005).
9. See USHUD (2004).
10. See Drever (1999).
11. See Kovaleski & Chan (2001).

CHAPTER 6

How Was the Research Conducted? Questioning Research Implementation

Numbers are created through the process of research. Based on the research questions, design, and subject selection, the **research implementation** activates the process of gathering and assessing data. In this context data refer to the numbers (though in other types of research, data could refer to other empirical codes) created in the process of translating ideas into empirical observations. In this chapter we consider questions that might be asked about how the research was conducted, based on an initial assessment of how key concepts are defined (described in the previous chapter). Once variables are conceptualized and operationalized, how do researchers acquire their data? How do they gain access? How do they document their observations? How do these decisions reflect and contribute to political concerns?

How Are Data Gathered?

Gathering data may involve observing people or texts, as well as asking questions through a variety of means. Researchers might evaluate a variety of social texts, representing productions of human creation ranging from television, film, and print content to **artifacts** such as graffiti, museum installations, or music. Researchers might also observe or query people, through participating in intentional experiences, observing conversations and behaviors, or asking questions to individuals or

groups. There are many ways to study people, ranging from direct observation and questioning to indirect reports on surveys or questionnaires.
How the researcher approaches the people being studied may have a
substantial influence on the data produced through that process.

Through **participant observation**, a researcher might work directly
with the research subjects, such as through joining teams, organizations, or other social groups, or watch subjects from a distance without
engaging in the activities of the group. The context of the site, along
with the researcher's ability to navigate the terrain and negotiate with
the community, contributes to potential access to research subjects. In
attempting to observe and count street homeless, many are missed, in
part due to hired counters feeling unsafe in studied areas late at night.[1]
The continuum of these modes of operation designate different ways of
gathering data, with one end emphasizing more participation, through
speaking and direct involvement, and the other more distanced observation. Observations of people constitute one central source of data, at
times combined with asking questions through interviews or surveys.

Interviewing subjects directly, whether through open-ended or
more structured formats, can focus on individual informants or on
groups, either through focus groups designated by the researcher or
small groups organized through the researchers' key informants. Surveys
of research subjects can also involve telephone contact, the Internet, or
paper, distributed through researchers directly or through other chan-
nels. Researchers might gather data through multiple methods but will
need to select approaches and implementation processes with particular
political implications in mind.

On similar subjects these approaches might produce widely
divergent results. Sometimes direct observations of what people do
may conflict with reports of what people admit through questioning. For example, documenting language use in public spaces through
observation produces different estimates than assessments based on
self-reports through surveys.[2] Considering consistent as well as divergent patterns across different approaches to gathering data adds depth
to our understanding. Combining approaches would add strength to
the research results.

It is worth questioning how data might have looked different if
they had been gathered in a different way. The reviewer should consider how the research results might have differed if the researchers
had asked directly rather than observed people; had asked people in

person or requested a response through the Internet; had posed open-ended or structured questions; or had even assured research subjects of anonymity instead of confidentiality (described later in this chapter). These decisions help determine the relative level of comfort and interest informants might have, which would affect the validity of the answers they might give. Also, some of these decisions might be seen as guiding potentially upper or lower limits of responses.

Observing people directly allows the researcher to document concrete conditions and actions, such as owning a cell phone or using one while driving; alternatively, asking people to self-report might lead to an over-estimation of cell phone possession (if seen as desirable) or an under-estimation of driving while talking on a cell phone (if seen as inappropriate). If the issue raised is seen as favorable, prestigious, or necessary, self-reporting may lead to an upper limit, while the converse would be true of conditions seen as less than socially acceptable. Direct observation also holds some limitations, however. If the observation is of direct behaviors, it may be difficult to understand if the research subject intends them as they are interpreted. A threatening punch on a playground might be intended as a joke rather than toward malicious harm. Similarly, Caucasian voters might claim to vote for African-American candidates in public opinion polls but then do otherwise when voting. Observing documentation, such as of vaccination records, would lead to a lower limit, given that people may lose papers or may not be able to find them. In contrast, asking parents about their children's vaccination status would lead to an upper limit, if having that done is seen as socially desirable.

The context through which people respond to interviews or surveys also guides and constrains the data produced. When asked directly, people may be forced to voice answers to issues they have little interest in or knowledge about, whereas giving people paper or a computer screen to record their answers might allow for more time in considering thoughtful responses. Without the researcher being directly involved, though, on paper or on a screen respondents might be able to skip questions more easily. Asking questions of informants as individuals also demands that they articulate particular responses given their own memories and experiences. Interviewing informants in groups, in contrast, might help inspire memories of experiences perhaps forgotten, or create a comfortable environment for admitting potentially controversial, sensitive, or illegal behavior, such as drinking alcohol and driving.

The nature of the questions asked also conditions the production of data. Clear, direct questions that ask about issues one at a time and suggest that recall be limited to more recent (such as yesterday) rather than distant experience are easier for informants to answer, and thus will produce more reliable and valid data. Phrasing questions in ways that allow informants to voice potentially controversial answers also will increase the likelihood of more divergent responses. In addition to how research questions are phrased, the format of potential answers also matters. If the format is open-ended, then the informant might have more flexibility in terms of interpretation of the ideas as well as the vocabulary used than if asked to reduce complex responses into simplistic answer formats. However, the open-ended format privileges the responses of those who have stronger opinions and interest in the subject; informants with less time or inclination may just leave the answer blank. Structured answers also lend toward more reliability, which was addressed in the previous chapter.

Research subjects might also be more comfortable providing answers to questions if they are informed of and understand a guarantee of **confidentiality** (when the researcher could divulge an informant's identity but promises not to do so) or of **anonymity** (when it is not possible to identify names with responses even if asked to do so). The latter is the more secure process for protecting the rights of informants. (These issues are addressed in more detail later in this chapter.) While it is clearly important to create these conditions of comfort and privacy when asking sensitive questions about illegal or perceived immoral behavior, many other answers will be conditioned by these factors as well, such as political attitudes and social prejudices, and even reported income and education.

How Do Researchers Gain Access to Data?

Access is an issue that matters to the study of people as well as of texts. How the researcher locates materials, solicits participation, or engages in observation should be described in the methodological description of the project. When studying texts, access may refer to the process of gaining permission (if needed), acquiring texts, and documenting observations. How data are acquired and how observations are documented depend on whether texts are considered within a public or private domain, as well as which agencies control their distribution. When reviewing descriptions of research approaches, the reviewer should consider the political contexts in which the researchers are attempting to acquire, store, and share information they gather about people as well as texts.

Social texts require access, which may require institutional authorization. Studies of television programs, films, newspaper coverage, and other media expressions when in the public domain rarely require formal permission when included in a textual analysis, yet permission might be needed if they are to be featured in focus group or other audience research. If the researcher relies on formal permission to review organizational records, the final selection of documents is restricted rather than representative of the broader set of written records. The reviewer should consider how researchers acquire access to the documents they study, and how these selections contribute to the nature of the data produced.

When researchers work with people, many questions need to be raised about the ways they have approached and informed research subjects as well as how they have documented and stored their information. One stage in this process involves gaining access to people to observe or to interview. In the process of gaining access, researchers may choose to confess or to conceal that they are conducting research. If the process is to be known, then the researchers need to identify potential risks as well as procedures for addressing them and must gain informed consent from research participants that they understand these risks and volunteer to be part of the process knowingly. Once the data are gathered, then researchers also need to decide how to document and store data to protect the rights and interests of the participants. Whether data can be traced to individual identities or not becomes part of the consideration of anonymity and confidentiality (see next section on how researchers document observations).

Some decisions made in the process of research are guided by a sense of what will produce valid results; yet ethical concerns also guide the process of research, particularly when studies focus on people as subjects. Researching people must begin with a fundamental respect for the health and dignity of all participating in the process of research—as subjects, as participants, and even as investigators. Research investigators hold power in the process of collecting data about people, and with this power comes responsibility. Agencies and individuals proposing, conducting, and presenting research have a responsibility to protect the rights of those in the researched community, as well as to respect their voices and visions.

Deception

Whether the researcher has engaged in covert activity to acquire documents or to observe people should be established in a description of the research process. When researchers deceive their subjects, hiding their intent to observe or to gather documents, ethical considerations need to transcend concerns with research validity. This is another area in which absolute rules are less apparent and situations demand thoughtful analysis.

Under what conditions is it appropriate for researchers to deceive people in the service of their work? Is it ever appropriate? This practice occurs in experiments, as well as through participant observations, when those conducting the research do not inform research subjects that they are in a study at all, or mislead them as to the actual subject of the research. Milgram's classic experimental research is often raised on this subject. In this experiment, 40 subjects were asked to administer electric shocks to participants if they answered questions incorrectly, not knowing that the people being "shocked" were acting and were not being physically harmed. The justification at the time was that this deception offered insight into individuals' potential to obey orders despite the harm they would inflict on others. Research participants may be harmed when they realize their capacities for aggression.[3]

In another classic illustration of deception, Humphreys' study of men having sex with men in public restrooms involved subsequent searching of their license plate numbers in order to chronicle demographic data, such as (heterosexual) marriage status. On the one hand this process of data collection potentially compromised private information that these men might not have wanted known; on the other hand, this research offered evidence that certain sexual acts were more widely practiced than among a self-declared homosexual community.[4] Researchers may attempt to justify deception by arguing that the knowledge gained outweighs the potential risks. They may also describe procedures used at the beginning or at the end of the observation period that might help guard against potential harm. Researchers might debrief research subjects, for example, explaining the actual purpose of the research and offering counseling or other services.

Reviewers should consider whether the researcher has engaged in deception in the process of gathering data, and whether this seems to be justified given the potential harm to participants in light of the potential knowledge gained from the study. Researchers should explain how the rights of informants have been protected, and confirm the ways in which potential harm has been addressed.

Voluntary Participation

When researchers do not engage in deception but openly request subjects' participation in research, the subjects should be told that they can choose whether or not to participate, and can stop participating at any time. To reinforce the voluntary nature of this transaction, researchers should clarify that there would be no penalty for refusal to participate. Yet how we perceive potential risks of noncompliance may depend on the relationship between potential participants and the people conducting the research. If professors ask students to volunteer to be in their studies, would the students feel concerned that refusal might affect their rapport with these professors? Would patients or prisoners involuntarily committed to institutions feel compelled to participate if requested by institutional authorities? The power difference within the institutional setting may make it difficult for the potential research subject to refuse without worrying about subsequent repercussions.

Some researchers argue that deception is an important way to study sensitive issues because it allows them to observe natural behavior. For example, we might get different results studying racist comments made through a virtual community if the research purpose is disclosed before data are gathered. An advantage to using deception in this case is that responses have more validity (see Chapter 5). However, individual rights to privacy might be compromised, depending on the perceived nature of the dialogue as part of a public or private space (addressed again later in this chapter), particularly given that researchers may be legally required to report certain types of statements to political authorities.

Informed Consent

Some researchers excuse deception as necessary to their research if they can verify that participants have given **informed consent** to be in the research and have had the actual purpose explained once the research was over. Researchers should stress to potential participants that the process is voluntary and should inform them of potential risks, of research subjects' rights, and of the processes used to maintain the anonymity or confidentiality of the information. As a first step the researcher shares this information, but that is not enough: participants must also acknowledge that they have understood this information and have agreed to the process.

Consent becomes the next step. Competent adults are considered able to consent, or agree to participate in the research study. Others, such as children, who are viewed not to have either the legal capacity or the ability to offer consent, instead offer assent, which is supplemented by the consent of an appropriate adult. Verification of informed consent requires written or verbal agreement, and the researcher must also establish that the participant is of an age to grant consent; this is not easily done through Internet or telephone interviews. While certain groups, such as minors, are protected from being part of a research process without the permission of their parents, in many other situations the rules are not so clear.

Procedures for acquiring informed consent are particularly important when researchers are studying private spaces, sensitive subjects, confidential information, or vulnerable groups. Conversely, some researchers might justify avoiding obtaining informed consent if they are studying people in public spaces, researching non-controversial topics, using anonymous information, or working with non-marginalized communities. Decisions about the nature of the research space, the topic's sensitivity, the ability to protect informants, and the vulnerability of the studied community are made in conjunction with collaborating organizations that fund and approve the research, as well as in consultation with colleagues and professional groups (see Chapter 2).

Public Space

Researchers may believe they can ignore procedures toward ensuring informed consent when research subjects are in a public setting. It is worth considering the specific nature of the research setting: Would it be appropriate for researchers to document what people are doing and saying without their knowledge? Does it matter if researchers are recording their observations with a video camera? Is it appropriate for researchers to collect statements made on public websites without informing participants that they are being observed? Answers to these questions may seem to depend on whether research subjects are being observed in a public or private space.

However, the distinction between public and private space is not always clear. While actual places may be designated as public (such as an open city park) or as private (such as inside a home), virtual spaces are more difficult to define. How Internet discussions become construed as a public or private setting is highly contingent on the historical and cultural context of the technology. North American researchers argue that in their context at this stage the Internet can be seen as "public," given that many people are familiar with the medium and are able to retain their anonymity with a pseudonym.[5] Another period of time or different community might have different expectations of and familiarity with this as a space for communication.

Another level to consider is whether participants expect their communication to be limited to restricted members or open to public view. The nature of the participants and their purpose for interaction might offer another level of a restricted access site worth considering. Participants discussing controversial or sensitive subjects might assume they are doing so with sympathetic comrades in a private setting. Researchers studying virtual spaces should describe whether the site operates as a public forum, such as Facebook, or with restricted access, such as the members-only chat group for survivors of sexual violence organized through the website www.aftersilence. org. In another example illustrating the importance of expectations, websites such as www.meshrep.com are designed to offer information as well as a space for public postings about the cultural heritage of the Uyghur community; however, Uyghur nationalists advocating for more sovereignty in territories such as the People's Republic of China would be more likely to restrict discussion to registered members.

How Do Researchers Document Their Observations?

Recording Observations

Analysis proceeds through the review of documented observations of texts or people, through written, audio, or visual records. If researchers record their observations on video cameras, then they may be assessing visual as well as verbal cues. If recording interviews on audiotape, then transcriptions of these verbal accounts might include attention to inflection, but most importantly would offer a complete record of each word said (if there are no technical difficulties). Recording notes on open-ended conversations or of observations on paper relies much more directly on the memory and patience of the researcher.

The reviewer should consider how the researchers have **documented** their observations. Would using alternative approaches to documentation have offered different kinds of information that would be pertinent to the research question? Whose permission was granted, if conversations were recorded? For instance, did researchers of an organization gain permission from organizational leaders or from lower-ranking constituents? Did the method of documentation enable the researcher to gather valid and reliable data? If field notes were taken, did this happen immediately following the researchers' experiences or interviews, or did enough time pass that you might question the accuracy of these written notes?

The validity of research participants' answers might also be related to whether they are informed that their information would be documented in a way to protect their privacy. Another critical decision in how to document observations addresses this very issue of protecting informants' responses.

Confidentiality and Anonymity

A central ethical concern is the potential identification of participants in connection with something they have said or done, recorded as research data. Researchers have choices to make in the process of data collection that could protect the anonymity of the participant, or ensure the confidentiality of this information.

With anonymity, it is not possible to connect recorded data with a particular individual. This not only helps to promote the validity of responses given (see Chapter 5), but can also be seen as the best way to protect the identity of the research informant. Whenever possible, researchers should separate identifying information as soon as they can. For example, researchers might maintain lists of addresses or telephone numbers that have been reached but not connect these to the specific surveys that have been completed. In this way each research participant's privacy is maintained. With groups who like using computers and want their information to be private, such as youths, anonymity can be protected by using computer-assisted self-interviewing systems to record responses.

However, it is not always possible to store data to achieve anonymity. When a researcher COULD expose an informant's identity but promises NOT to do so, data are kept in confidential form. For example, audio- and video-recorded interviews may allow informants' voices or faces to be identified. Web-based or emailed questionnaires might also be traceable to particular addresses. In these cases, researchers intend to keep responses confidential, through both the storage of data as well as the presentation of results.

Confidentiality becomes particularly important when divulging identities might cause research informants harm. If participants are being asked about illicit behavior or critical attitudes, then their admission becomes a political risk. Researchers studying illegal cannabis use among Aboriginal communities in Australia dealt with this concern by ensuring confidentiality in the local language as well as avoiding direct questions about specific illegal behavior.[6] In places where critiques against governments risk incarceration and torture, confidentiality is imperative. Victims of violence may also require confidentiality in order to feel safe.[7] The underlying issue here is concern for the long-term safety and well-being of people participating in the research project.

The problem with confidentiality is that broader political imperatives might jeopardize the privacy of informants. Researchers may be subject to court subpoena; in one example of this, Exxon requested a research team to provide confidential data that included informants' personal information about alcohol use, violence, and other psychological conditions to support Exxon's court case in Alaska.[8] In another case, a graduate student studying an animal rights movement endured 16 weeks in jail for not revealing the identities of his research informants. Although he was not suspected of participating in the destruction of property credited to animal rights activists, he was asked to share information gained through confidential interviews. His refusal to do so was based in part on the American Sociological Association's stated code of ethics that scholars maintain confidentiality of sources even when not legally protected.[9]

Scholars may also find themselves at legal risk given the political climate in which they work. For example, a sociologist working on ethnic conflict in the Congo was tortured and detained without trial for over eight months,[10] a political scientist studying Colombia's political factions faced an assassination attempt, and a marine biologist was accused by the Ukrainian government of exposing state secrets. The hundreds of scholars applying for assistance from the Scholars at Risk program attests to the political risk researchers face in many different countries.[11]

Why Research Implementation Matters

Research numbers represent artifacts created through the production of research. These specific processes shape and guide this construction, from the measurement of constructs through the process of gaining access to and documenting research data. While the phrasing of questions may determine the type and nature of answers given in the course of research, so too does the nature of implementation. Particularly with potentially sensitive subjects, informants might respond quite differently if asked questions about sexual abuse or rape directly in person, alone or in a group, over the telephone, through a website, or on paper. Given the discrepancies between the incidence of violent acts and willingness to report victimization, we would also expect differences in observing documented cases of rape and abuse in comparison with requesting self-reports. The incidence of sexual violence is much higher when assessed through nationally representative telephone surveys in the United States (1 in 59 adults) compared with cases reported and documented with public authorities.[12] While at times the problem may lie in the social stigma of reporting particular acts, in other situations police authorities may not be documenting violent acts in ways that chart group prejudice. Despite a recent concern with anti-Semitism in the United Kingdom, documented through surveys, police authorities are not recording these acts. While the U.S. FBI does document crimes against Jews in the country as a whole, states have widely divergent definitions for hate crimes.[13]

How researchers record observations and interviews also contributes to the production of data. Some documentation strategies facilitate recording whether informants exhibited signs of discomfort with certain topics, perhaps pausing, laughing nervously, or looking off into the distance. Audio and video complements to written records may supplement nonverbal cues that might help explain aspects of the research implementation and might contribute to research findings.

The format of answers can also lead to problematic results. Researchers going through the 2000 census believe that 40 percent of same-sex "unmarried" couples are actually different-sex couples who are misclassified because of problematic formatting of questions.[14] Given the political controversy over the legal definition of marriage, documenting the prevalence of different types of unions matters.

Creating services and advocating policies to address social issues depends on understanding the context in which problems occur. Resource allocation to serve homeless populations depends upon an estimation of the size and composition of this group, though this enumeration proves particularly difficult. A variety of data sources and implementation plans produce quite varied results. Indirect methods, such as using shelter service data, along with interviews with key informants, tend to offer higher estimates, particularly when compared with attempts at counting this population through direct observations and interviews, which produces lower estimates.[15]

If the purpose of research is to explore possibilities and to acquire knowledge in the service of the public good, then the benefits of the research must outweigh any possible harm. This includes not just physical harm, but also psychological and emotional harm, such as discomfort and anxiety, either through the process of conducting research or in the subsequent presentation of results. For example, although participants in a clinical medical experiment might not experience physical harm, being deceived by medical professionals might risk their future trust in the medical community. How the potential contribution of the research contrasts with the potential risks is determined by a constellation of communities and institutions with power to fund, regulate, and implement the research (see Chapter 2).

There are ways to engage in a research process that might create possibilities for research *subjects* to become more involved as research *participants*. "Action research" is an approach to the research process that begins with this principle as a moral imperative: research participants should have control over the purpose and process of the research, relative to the researchers. While action research is one particular approach to the process of research as a whole, other steps, such as ensuring anonymity, contribute to a potentially more respectful and responsible process of working with people in the process of data collection.

The numbers produced through the research process are contingent upon these processes of implementation, from the very definitions of the issues to how observations are gathered, recorded, and prepared for analysis. Next, we need to consider what we know through analysis and interpretation of research findings.

Key Terms

Anonymity

Confidentiality

Deception

Informed Consent

Interviewing

Participant Observation

Research Access

Research Documentation

Research Implementation

Social Artifact

Review Questions

1. How are data gathered?
2. How do researchers gain access to data?
3. How do researchers document observations?
4. What strategies are used to protect research subjects?

Reflection Questions

1. How do researchers have power over those who are the subjects of research?
2. How can the implementation process offer research subjects more control over the data collected?
3. Are there any conditions that might justify the use of deception in the research process?
4. Would you be willing to go to jail to protect your sources of information?

Exercise

Find someone willing to participate in this exercise with you, offering confidentiality and recognition that the information gathered will be used only for class purposes. Pick a topic that will allow for easy public observation, such as listening to music, eating habits, or studying rituals. Observe these patterns and record your observations. Next, interview your research subject, and then compare your observations with her or his self-reports.

Follow this exercise then in reverse, allowing your informant to become the researcher. After your partner observes you, have him or her interview you on the subject of the observation. Listen to what your partner has observed about you, and consider how your own understanding of your actions relates to how you answer questions on the topic. Consider how a researcher offering you anonymity might change your answers. Reflect on whether you believe a researcher would be justified in using deception to collect observations on the subject of your exercise.

Notes

1. See Farrell & Reissing (2004).
2. See Urla (1993).
3. See Milgram (1965).
4. See Humphreys (1970).
5. See Pittenger (2003).
6. See Clough & Conigrave (2008).
7. See Yick (2007).
8. Reviewed in Babbie (2004), among other research methods texts.
9. See Monaghan (1993).
10. See Rossouw (2002).
11. See McMurtrie (2003).
12. See Basile et al. (2007).
13. See Iganski (2007).
14. See Black et al. (2007).
15. See Drever (1999); NCH (2005); USHUD (2004).

....

CHAPTER 7

What Do We Know? Questioning Analysis and Interpretation

In this chapter, we consider what we can know based on the reported research results. When research fits a more explanatory model, analyses may include analyses across several variables, building on descriptions of individual variables. Reviewing results helps build a case for what we know as a consequence of the research, as well as what we still do not know but should know given the social problem motivating the research.

What Do We Know about Patterns across Variables?

Once individual measures have been assessed as reliable and valid, then analyses testing connections across these variables can begin if moving from an exploratory or descriptive to an explanatory approach. Analyses might then consider patterns of results across variables, as well as tests of significance and strength (reviewed in the next section).

It is worth noting the type of analytical tools researchers use, as well as their processes of analysis. Categorized observations may be processed through a variety of statistical approaches. Statistical software packages might be used in this process, such as the Statistical Package for the Social Sciences (SPSS). Some research projects rely on primary data, collected for the purpose of that study, while others use secondary data that have been gathered by others for different purposes. Meta-analysis, for example, relies on secondary data, incorporating many studies on a similar topic in order to establish patterns.

First, patterns of results are assessed in relation to projected hypotheses or questions guiding the research. Working deductively, analyses are designed to test given hypotheses or to answer specific questions, examining patterns speculated in advance. If we hypothesize that women might be more likely to watch films than men, then we would correlate gender with film viewing. Working inductively, we might instead explore how gender might correlate with a variety of media habits, without suggesting in advance women's preferences or habits. Whether working deductively or inductively, the process of analysis relies on observations of patterns. How large the difference is between women and men in terms of their preferences for particular film genres, for example, attests to the degree of strength (reviewed in the next section) between gender and media interests.

Observing patterns in analysis involves a process of considering similarities and differences across variables. Many different analytical tools might be used to illustrate **bivariate** (across two variables) or multivariate (across more than two) patterns. Many of the analytical tools considered to hold statistical strength (reviewed in the next section) require having interval-level or ratio-level variables. If there is a political need to establish strong evidence of a pattern, then variables may need to be measured initially in this way or recoded in a way to allow for regression and similar types of analyses to be used. We might record number of hours watching television, for example, to take advantage of these analytical procedures, instead of asking respondents to circle ordinal categories such as never, sometimes, often, always. Alternatively, ordinal categories, such as those used in agree/disagree scales, could be recoded into interval-level form.

Analyses build on visual observations across patterns of numbers, which might be shown as percentages in **cross-tabulations** or means in analyses of variance. For example, researchers might compare the percentage of women in a study reading newspapers compared to the percentage of men, or compare the average number of television hours watched across age groups. Percentages should be presented because they may depict a different pattern than absolute numbers. For example, while the absolute number of people with health insurance in the United States increased between 2004 and 2005, the percentage of people WITHOUT health insurance increased, given population estimates.[1] Absolute numbers also give a very different picture than do percentages in the case of foreign aid: in terms of the amount of aid disbursed from bilateral organizations, the United States is the largest donor; however, when calculating the amount of aid given as a percentage of gross national income, then Sweden offers the most foreign aid.[2]

Information on patterns may be presented through verbal descriptions in the text, as well as through numbers in tables and charts. When reviewing tables and charts, the reader should take note of the total numbers presented as well as the percentages given. The first step is to consider the total number of people or artifacts used to create the table, and to compare this to the total number in the sample. If the numbers do not match, the reviewer should determine what the number in the table represents. Which part of the sample is excluded? For example, if a table describes attitudes among 200 respondents but 300 were surveyed, why 100 were left out? It may be that the latter group of 100 did not answer that question, were neutral on the topic, or were filtered out for not owning a television or watching television.

When percentages are given, the reviewer should also note what the denominator represents. Percentages of Internet use take on different meanings, for example, whether constructed as a proportion of all users or within a group that includes non-users. To illustrate, estimates of Internet use in Asia reach about 15 percent of the regional population, yet in another percentage this group represents more than a third of all global users; and while about three-quarters of those in North America are considered Internet users, this group represents under one-fifth of the global user community.[3] Understanding how percentages are calculated is critical to interpreting the results given.

Next, the reviewer should consider how the percentages compare with each other across the independent variable. Typically an independent variable will be presented along an x axis, with column percents used to contrast patterns across a dependent variable. For example, we might see a table comparing the percentage of women participating in marathon competitions compared to the percentage of men. If there is no difference between them, these percentages should be the same. The reviewer should note the degree to which these percentages differ. For example, in response to an alleged concern that European Muslim communities are more likely to identify with their religious affiliation than with their nation, we could refer to survey results demonstrating that most Muslim respondents in London, Paris, and Berlin identify with both the country where they live (73 percent in London, 74 percent in Paris, and 72 percent in Berlin) as well as with their religious identity

(88 percent in London, 68 percent in Paris, and 85 percent in Berlin).[4] We could examine the percentage differences within each city and conclude that most identify with both nation and religion, or that there seems to be a slight (between 6 and 15 percent) difference between these allegiances, but the direction differs across city.

Visual representations of data can be used to emphasize particular positions. The scale of presentation used on a figure can serve to accentuate a small difference or—if changed to include a broader range—to downplay a difference in percentages. The following figures help to illustrate how difference in scale serves to accentuate possible interpretations. In Figure 1a, estimates of poverty across region and over time are displayed over several regions with some variation across region as well as over time. In contrast, Figure 1b focuses only on the Latin American/ Caribbean and Middle East/North African regions. With a more narrow range along the axis depicting the millions living in poverty, the differences between these two regions and over time are more accentuated than they are in the first figure with a broader range.[5] The numbers used in these figures are meant to demonstrate how visual shifts in parameters may help focus interpretation, but it is worth reiterating an earlier

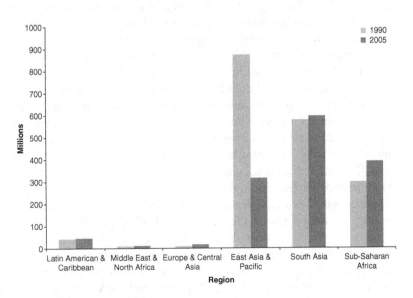

FIGURE 1A Poverty Across Regions 1990 & 2005

point that it is also worth knowing the percentages of people living in poverty within a population, and not just absolute numbers.

The reviewer should also note the percentages that are used in verbal descriptions of observed patterns. How similar or different do groups appear on the variables that matter most to the analysis? To establish the degree to which these percentages or means might be similar or different, statistics are used to assess the significance and strength or the observed patterns.

Significance

Statistical significance is assessed through analytical procedures agreed upon by communities of researchers; policy significance, on the other hand, is determined in relation to current debate by political advocates and agencies. While these assessments are created through different types of groups and through different processes, the establishment of statistical significance helps those advocating particular policy positions to assert their points based on empirical data.

More specifically, statistical significance refers to the degree to which results are believed to have occurred by chance. This assessment technically refers to the degree to which a particular sample is

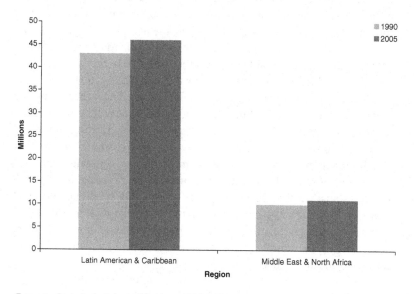

FIGURE 1B **Poverty in Selected Regions 1990 & 2005**

expected to reflect the patterns of a broader population, and thus should be restricted to probability random sampling strategies (see Chapter 4). This is the first step in statistically establishing a pattern worth noting. If significance figures are used with sampling strategies that do not use probability selection procedures, then the statistics used will have little relevance.

Researchers are able to control two factors contributing to the assertion of significance. First, the calculation of these statistics is based on sample size, assuming a random selection of people or artifacts from a known population. If a sample is relatively small, even dramatic patterns may not show up as statistically significant, whereas large samples connote significance with even the slightest differences. If we observe, for example, that 75 percent of children who are heavy television viewers exhibit violent tendencies compared with 50 percent of children who are light viewers, this might seem like a large difference, but the significance of the difference would depend on the sample size. If the total sample includes 12 children, then this might not be significant, but if the sample was as large as 1200, then it would. The chi square calculation is used to determine the probability statistic. The chi square formula relates the observed number to the expected number in a given table cell, squared, divided by the expected number in that cell. The sample size determines how large that expected number might be, changing the chi square value considerably when the sample is large or small. The overall chi square value of the table is determined as a sum of these values figured for each table cell, and then added together to determine a level of significance, reported as a p value in a table or text.

If there is a political need to establish significance, then sampling large groups through random sampling techniques will be more likely to produce significant results. The Legacy Media Tracking Survey of almost 33,000 teens may seem excessive in comparison to many other telephone surveys evaluating health communication campaigns, but this abundance of research subjects contributes to the potential for demonstrating statistical significance.[6] On the other hand, small incidences of crime, even though not statistically significant, become sensationalized in media coverage, contributing to our perceived sense of risk.[7] In sum, by enhancing the sample size, researchers are more likely to be able to assert significant results.

The other factor within the researchers' control is the decision to set the level of statistical significance. It is typically set at .05, which means that researchers believe that there is less than a 5 percent probability that the observed results have occurred by chance ($p < .05$). Establishing significance at this level is arbitrary but is assumed as appropriate based on conventional wisdom as established by groups of researchers. Other levels, such as establishing significance at a more conservative $p < .01$ level or a more permissive $p < .10$ level, might also be used, again depending on the rules established through the practices of a research community. Changing this level of significance might work depending on the approval granted or denied by the research community.

Strength

Separate from significance, other statistics are used to establish the **strength** of a **correlation**, documenting the degree to which one variable is associated with another. Correlation statistics do not depend on sample size, but instead assess degrees of difference across observed numbers. Selecting these statistics depends on the nature of measurement used: some require interval- or ratio-level data while others work with nominal- or ordinal-level categories. While the latter variables are more limited in the types of statistics that can be used, the interval- and ratio-level measures can use a full range of statistics. The more advanced the measurement (ratio being the most and nominal being the least), the more analytical tools the researcher has to select from, including those considered to have the most weight given the legitimacy accorded by the social science community. Researchers may need to take into account the analytical and by implication political strength when assessing the consequences of their measurement choices. For example, we could measure amount of television viewing by asking respondents to check never, sometimes, often (as an ordinal measure) or to write the number of hours watched yesterday (as a ratio measure). The ratio-level measure would allow researchers to use regression and other more complex statistical techniques that would not be permissible with ordinal- or nominal-level data.

In practice, we can examine many different possible statistics assessing the strength of relationships across variables. At times some of these statistics suggest more strength than others, giving the researcher some choice. Again, the dictates of the research community rather than the whim of the researcher guide this choice.

The statistics used to assess strength generally vary from −1 to 0 to 1. Reading a 0 to represent strength would mean that there was absolutely no difference between the groups. If 30 percent of an urban community wore hats compared with 30 percent of those in a suburban community, then the strength would be documented at 0. If, however, all of the urban community wore hats but none of those living in the suburbs did, then the strength would be 1, or –1, depending on which group was listed first. Given that most data do not result in such complete similarities or differences, the strength statistic gives some sense of how different the percentages are. The strength statistic may be represented by a number following an r. The closer the statistic is to a complete 1.0 or –1.0, the stronger the relationship. However, researchers can look at the same statistic, such as $r = .4$, and say that this demonstrates either little strength or moderate strength.

Causality

Whether **causality** can be attributed to results depends upon the agreement of researchers to a particular set of rules. These rules suggest first the need to establish correlation and then temporal order, such that it is clear that one variable precedes the other. For example, we assume age conditions media use rather than the other way around. It may not be clear, though, whether media use leads to political attitudes or whether attitudes condition selection of media, so that in this case temporal order cannot be established. The first two criteria can be readily argued, depending on the observed statistics and assumptions made about the phenomena measured. The third condition, however—that no other alternative explanation exists—becomes more difficult to establish. Given a more humble approach to research, there are always other conditions or factors that might help explain results. Within certain research communities, then, causality is never established. Yet in others, when there is a political need to do so, the word "causal" might be included in an interpretation to assert strength to the results.

What Do We Still Need to Know?

Having established the results of the research, the reviewer should consider how else the findings might be explained. What alternative reasons might explain these results? The authors might hint at other possible explanations in a concluding section considering what future research should be conducted. We might also consider factors or conditions that the authors have not acknowledged. Factors might include other characteristics that might precede or intervene between the independent and dependent variables, such as gender, age, class, lifestyle, or disposition. Conditions might refer to particular historical events or periods, long-term trends, geographical or spatial circumstances, political-economic structures, or sociocultural contexts. Research continues as a long-term process, rather than as a distinct isolated project, as we explore alternative explanations for what it is we believe we know.

Thinking about **alternative interpretations** means considering a variety of explanations for and extensions of initial results. If we limit our attention to the finding that the number of global refugees has declined over time, from 15 million in 1995 to 12 million in 2002, we might suggest limiting resources and attention to this as a central social problem. But Crisp's analysis illustrates that another 25 million people have been displaced but were not eligible for this count because they migrated against their will within their national boundaries.[8]

In another example, a recent study of university students chronicled the political orientations of university students from freshmen to senior year to assess the degree to which professors might be influencing students' professed political sentiments.[9] A number of findings are apparent in one particular table reported in a press release of this academic article in *PS: Political Science and Politics*. First, the argument that many hoped to make is that college students are indoctrinated by professors' supposedly liberal leanings. These data show that there is a slight shift from freshman (when 1.6 percent identify as far left and 23.3 percent as liberal) to senior year (3.6 percent as far left and 29.1 percent as liberal). Yet, we could also point to the slight difference between seniors and the larger cohort of 18-to-24-year-olds to suggest that university students are not all that different from others their age (comparing seniors to the broader cohort, 3.6 percent and 5.3 percent identify as far left, 29.1 percent and 28.7 percent as liberal, 23.6 percent and 23.4 percent as conservative, and 0.9 percent and 2.1 percent as far right). Another distinction evident within the table that was not picked up in the news coverage of the study is the sharp difference between college students' identification as moderate (47.8 percent of freshman and 42.8 percent of seniors) in relation to that of the broader population (38.3 percent). It may be that the effect of education is to produce more moderate political sentiments overall rather than to encourage leftist attitudes. Or, those with moderate political orientations may be more likely to attend private universities, which were the focus of this study.

After considering a variety of alternative reasons that might explain what we do know based on the research, we can then venture into broader questions, addressing what we still do not know. On a specific level, we can question what is still not known within the parameters of the research itself. Results may have pointed in directions other than those hypothesized, or may have further muddied simplified expectations. When expectations in research are not met, this allows for further reflection on what is still not known.

Beyond the parameters of the research project, there is much still to be known about the subject under investigation. Considering the concluding remarks given about the research project, and the topic more broadly, what is still not known that should be known? How would this contribute to future research projects?

If the research project is considered as a whole, in light of its social justification, through what other ways could this subject be studied? By thinking creatively through each of the sets of issues in research, there are many possible ways to explore a topic. How would a different research design, such as an experimental, longitudinal, cross-sectional, or case study approach, offer different types of logics to this subject? How would different sampling strategies influence the external validity of what we know? How would different sources and approaches to data contribute to our observations? These questions lead to further considerations of how different approaches to analysis and presentations of data might shift attention from other potential interpretations.

Why Analysis and Interpretation Matter

Interpretations of research results can vary, and the results themselves are a product of the decisions made in the course of analysis. While many decisions are made in the process of designing, implementing, and analyzing research that contribute to the production of numbers, the act of interpretation involves an inherently social and political process as well. With interpretation, researchers propose an explanation for the importance of the numbers produced through research, which may then be reframed through public debate on issues.

The art of interpretation carries political consequences in determining how we explain our world. For instance, judicial and public debate on the potential inclusion of "intelligent design" in public school science classes raises the issue of what constitutes "science" as well as how we consider interpreting all that we do not know in our explanations of natural as well as social worlds. A central feature of this discussion concerns how the reasoning of intelligent design operates outside the parameters of scientific procedures and assumptions.[10] The politics of this reasoning hinges on what are considered appropriate modes of interpretation. Interpretation may also be seen as guided by a political interest in asserting a position on an issue. For example, Texas has spent more and has received more federal funds than any other state on abstinence-only programs in public school sex education, but it has one of the highest teen birth rates in the country.[11] While this paradox can be used to advocate for more comprehensive educational programs, the East Texas Abstinence Program on ESTEEM (Encouraging Students To Embrace Excellent Marriage) counters that the teen birth rate in the state has actually declined since 1991.[12]

These data become used in a variety of ways to argue for presenting more narrowly focused or more broadly focused sex education information to children in public schools. Although most poll data demonstrate that most respondents support more comprehensive sex education programs, the U.S. Congress has supported more than two decades worth of abstinence-only projects costing more than $1 billion, despite the lack of empirical evidence that these educational programs result in teens waiting any longer than they would have otherwise to initiate sexual contact. Population scholars view abstinence-only education as a social movement that rejects science, damaging the health of individuals in an effort to control women's sexuality.[13] As in the debate over intelligent design, interpretation is tied not only to political position but also to a sense of what constitutes a scientific process of analysis.

News coverage of social science research tends to emphasize the more controversial analyses that resonate with current political arguments. During the height of U.S. media attention to Rev. Wright's sermons, for instance, issues of race and religion were more pronounced in political discussions. Given this political context, among the many analyses conducted through the Pew Research Center public opinion poll in March 2008,[14] media focused mostly on those findings assessing public attention and assessment of Wright's sermons, then-candidate Barack Obama's response, and the public misperception of Obama as Muslim (the oft-quoted statistic being one in ten Americans).[15]

Moreover, public debate can selectively highlight data compatible with asserted claims within more complex results. Extensive studies on the effects of violence in the media have produced varying results, mostly confirming the concerns of advocacy groups but also supporting the defenses of the entertainment industry. Bushman and Anderson's[16] analysis of news coverage of scholarship on media violence and aggression demonstrate that over time, media coverage highlights claims toward statistical strength or weakness, despite the nature of the research evidence. They point out that while major professional groups, such as the American Psychological Association and the American Medical Association, publicly condemn media violence as contributing to aggression among children, industry representatives trivialize these research findings as statistically weak. While the correlations have been demonstrated across research projects, the interpretation of the importance of these findings is grounded in the institutional agenda of the organization, whether in the realm of advocating for children's health or in defending profit-driven entertainment.

When evidence seems to diverge from conventional wisdom, research tends to be questioned even more. Recent longitudinal research on television programming demonstrates that over time most forms of sexual content have decreased, yet the discourse of advocates, politicians, industry representatives, and even academics supports the idea that we are seeing more sexual content now than in the past.[17] And despite clear correlations between exposure to pornography and desensitization to and abuse of women, groups loyal to this industry discount the strength and breadth of these research findings.[18]

Numbers are not merely reported but also interpreted through written and oral presentations. When the numbers help illustrate politically palatable arguments, numbers tend to be asserted as evidence. Conversely, when numbers appear confusing or contradictory with particular interests, then they are more likely to be characterized as less than legitimate, perhaps through critiques of the particular research or through skepticism toward research in general. The credibility of the research process in many senses becomes contingent upon how the observed results fare in relation to expectations.

Key Terms

Alternative Interpretations
Bivariate Analysis
Causality
Correlation

Cross-tabulation
Statistical Significance
Strength

Review Questions

1. What do we know about patterns across variables?
2. Do results establish statistical significance? Strength?
3. What do we still need to know?

Reflection Questions

1. Given the methodological advantages of large sample sizes, why would some research projects rely on smaller samples?
2. Why do some research subjects attract more controversy than others?

Exercise

Find a research study with clearly explained results. Consider alternative explanations for the results presented.

Notes

1. See DeNavas-Walt et al. (2005).
2. See World Bank (2009).
3. See Data360 (2009).
4. See Nyiri (2007).
5. These data on poverty represent the share of populations living on less than US $1.25 a day, estimated in 1990 and 2005. These figures are published in the World Bank's 2009 second edition of the *Atlas of Global Development*, pp. 20–21.
6. See Niederdeppe et al. (2007).
7. See Gandy (2010).
8. See Crisp (2003).
9. See Inside Higher Ed (2008).
10. See Chang (2005); Goodstein (2005); Orr (2005).
11. See Quindlen (2009).
12. Phan (2009) asserted that the teen birth rate among 15-to-17-year-olds had decreased by 43 percent, according to the East Texas Abstinence Program.
13. The January 2007 Conference on Human Rights, Cultural, and Scientific Aspects of Abstinence-Only Policies and Programs, sponsored by the Heilbrunn Department of Population and Family Health at Columbia University, William and Flora Hewlett Foundation, was devoted to this topic. This is summarized in Santellis & Kantor (2008).

14. See Pew Research Center (2008).
15. See AP (2008).
16. See Bushman & Anderson (2001).
17. See Hetsroni (2007).
18. See Jensen (2007).

....

Questioning Research

This final chapter is devoted to a summary of questions that could be posed in the process of reading research, particularly research that uses numbers in its presentation of data. Moving from reading to the act of critique means positioning the research within its political context, in terms of its funding and design, its implementation, and then its distribution and use in society.

Guideline of Questions

The following questions chronicle those explored in Chapters 2 through 7. This list should be used as a guideline of potential issues. Which questions have more salience will depend on the particular research studies reviewed.

Questioning the Research Context

The first set of questions deals with the context in which the research was initiated. These questions ask us to describe which organizations were involved in designing, funding, doing, and approving the research, as well as their reasons for doing so.

- What is the purpose of the research?
- Who designed the research?
- Who did the research?
- Who paid for the research?
- Who approved the research?
- What motivated each of these groups?

Questioning the Research Design

The next set of questions pertains to the design of the research. Once the actual design of the study has been identified (as experimental, comparative across time or groups, or case study), then the potential threats to internal validity can be assessed. These might concern the selection of people into groups or changes over time that make comparative designs suspect.

- What is the research design?
- What are the internal validity concerns with that design?
- How does the research design and its limitations relate to political interests in this subject?

Questioning Selection Strategies

Questioning how things or people are selected for research can address the logic of external validity issues, as well as the ethics of working with the designated group, particularly when vulnerable populations are the subject of research.

- What is the subject of the research?
- How are subjects selected?
- What are the limitations of the sample?
- How do selection strategies relate to political interests in this subject?

Questioning Key Terms

In addition to questioning the subject of the research as a source of data, another set of questions addresses what the research is about. We need to consider how the central terms are defined broadly and specifically structure the data gathered in the course of research.

- How are key concepts defined?
- How are variables operationalized from concepts?
- What do we know about key variables?
- How do definitions relate to political interests in this subject?

Questioning the Research Implementation

The data produced in the course of research can be acquired in many different ways, such as direct observation, asking questions, or reviewing documents. Moreover, we need to understand the process through which researchers gain access to and record their observations.

- How are data gathered?
- How do researchers gain access to data?
- How do researchers protect the privacy and rights of research informants?
- How do researchers document their observations?
- How does the research implementation relate to political interests in this subject?

Questioning Analysis and Interpretation

Finally, we should question the results presented. We can consider the patterns established across key variables in the research in terms of statistical significance and policy relevance as well as strength of correlations. We can also assess the visual representations of these patterns.

- What do we know about patterns across variables?
- What do we know from visual representations of data?
- How else could results be interpreted to support other political interests in this subject?

Why the Political Context Matters

As a next step toward critique, reading research through the guidelines presented above can be considered in a broader context, taking into account the political interests of those involved in the creation, the implementation, and the use of the research.

First, the political context of the agencies involved in the funding, implementation, and approval of the research needs to be situated within their own institutional interests. How does each of the groups involved in the research process justify this project, in light of their broader institutional goals?

Understanding the political motivations may help in terms of assessing the potential of the design and sampling strategies in addressing political interests. If, for example, organizations need to establish the effectiveness of an intervention with a strong research study, then they may be more interested in experimental or well-designed quasi-experimental research, selecting research participants using random procedures. If robust internal validity and external validity are necessary for future approval of a program or allocation of funds, then this should be reflected as such. The political context of implementation also suggests considering ways in which the definitions of key terms, along with the ways of collecting data, might correspond with these political interests. Finally, the context in which research is interpreted and understood, as well as the way in which it might be distributed, relates to the utility of the numbers in the broad political context. In the process of interpretation, we should consider not only what is known based on the research presented, but also what we still need to know in order to advocate for or question a political interest.

Numbers are used to advance and to resist political arguments in decisions and policies that matter directly in our lives. If numbers are to be understood and questioned as forms of legitimate evidence, then we must ask questions. The ultimate goal in questioning research using numbers is not toward dismissal or adoration, but toward respect and praxis. As part of a process of dialogue and action, praxis depends on a critical understanding of research numbers.

Anonymity: Research participants cannot be identified or connected with research data, protecting them from potential political consequences.

Attrition: From the researcher's point of view, if research subjects are no longer participating in the research, they are dead to the research project, so data over time are not comparable.

Bivariate Analysis: These analyses involve observing patterns across two variables, often presented in tables and through correlations (see **Strength**) to assess a relationship between them. This research is done when the purpose of the research is to explain a condition or event.

Case Study Design: This approach examines a particular event, situation, or condition in depth, allowing more attention to detail but less strength in an ability to explain for political purposes.

Causality: Politically there may be pressure to establish causality through research, which would mean demonstrating correlation, time order, and no alternative explanations for findings. However, verifying this third condition is difficult, so causality may be claimed without substantial evidence to do so.

Cohort Study: A population is studied over time as a cohort, although the particular members of the research study within the cohort may be different at each time of data collection. This model allows for comparisons over time.

Conceptualization: The process through which abstract ideas are defined in order to help focus the research.

Confidentiality: Although researchers claim that they will not identify particular research participants, it would be possible to do so given how data are collected if requested by a political agency.

Contamination: This occurs when a group in a research study gets enough of the intervention or treatment designated for the study group so that the groups are no longer comparable.

Control Group: When research participants are randomly assigned to receive an experimental intervention, participants in another group, designated as a control group, do not receive this intervention for comparison purposes.

Convenience Sampling: Researchers select people or things to study in a non-purposive, non-random way, taking advantage of opportunities.

Correlation: This descriptive statistic measures the strength across observed patterns of variables. The closer the number presented is to 1 or –1, the stronger the correlation is assumed to be. These statistics rely on interval- or ratio-level data.

Cross-Sectional Design: With this design groups of people or groups of artifacts are compared at one point in time.

Cross-tabulation: This presentation of variables in a table allows us to see patterns in two or more variables visually.

Deception: In the process of data collection, researchers may not explain to research participants that they are actually in a research study or may not explain the real intention of the study.

Deductive Process: In this approach to research, the process begins with broad ideas that become more narrowly focused to more concrete hypotheses to be tested in analysis.

Descriptive Research: This research approach is used to document conditions or events.

Evaluation Research: This research is designed to monitor or assess the effects of a social intervention.

Experimental Design: This design randomly assigns participants into groups experiencing different conditions.

Explanatory Research: This research approach is used to analyze patterns in two or more variables in order to explicate the subject of the study.

Exploratory Research: This research approach is used to study new trends or issues.

External Validity: This aspect of validity concerns whether results can be generalized across subjects, in other places, or at other times. In addition, experimental research may be seen as having low external validity given the artificial nature of the participants' experiences in contrast to more natural conditions.

Focus Groups: A facilitator guides research participants through a group interview process.

History: This threat to internal validity is considered with trends in longitudinal designs that might occur as a product of historical context, rather than due to the conditions being studied.

Inductive Process: In this approach to research, the process begins with a concrete observation and moves toward the consideration of more broadly based theories.

Informed Consent: Research participants agree to be part of a research project after having been informed of the risks involved.

Institutional Review Board: These and other agencies study research plans with a view toward safeguarding the rights of research subjects.

Instrumental Value: Numbers may have practical applications, such as allowing social services to plan to accommodate a particular number of clients.

Instrumentation: This threat to internal validity matters when a research instrument, such as a survey, survey words, or interviewer, changes over time and thus results are not comparable.

Internal Validity: This validity refers to design issues that may have influenced the results such that observed data might not be attributed to the designated condition or independent variable.

Inter-subjectivity: An epistemological approach that privileges the social and political construction of knowledge (we learn through socialization, which itself corresponds within a political world) over the idea of absolute objective knowledge (facts exist) or individual subjectivity (my perception is all I know).

Interval: Answers to questions may be categorized in ways that have equal distances between them.

Interviewing: In this process of data collection, research subjects are asked directly about their opinions and experiences.

Intrinsic value: An assumption that an object contains its own characteristics separate from human perception.

Level of Measurement: Categories used to describe answers to questions, in terms of nominal-, ordinal-, interval-, and ratio-level formats. These levels of measurement matter because they determine the kind of statistical analysis that can be used.

Longitudinal Design: With this design, data are collected over time for comparison.

Maturation: This threat to internal validity involves trends in longitudinal designs when findings might be attributed to people growing in maturity rather than the condition being studied.

Mean: This descriptive statistic is determined by dividing the sum of values over the number of observations. Because this calculation is susceptible to outliers, it may offer a misleading assessment of a condition.

Measurement Validity: This validity refers to whether what is being observed accurately reflects what researchers had intended to measure.

Median: This descriptive statistic reflects a middle value in rank order, being less susceptible to a few deviant cases than the mean statistic.

Mode: This descriptive statistic expresses the most frequently observed responses to a given question.

Nominal: A list of answers that has no meaningful order to them.

Non-Probability Sampling: In this selection process, research subjects or artifacts are selected in ways that are convenient or purposive and thus are not representative of any broader population. These sampling techniques may have less political strength because they have low external validity.

Numerical Literacy: This literacy refers to both a set of skills learned in order to understand numerical data as well as the use of these skills toward active critique.

Objectivity: An approach to understanding reality that assumes knowledge created through a scientific process exists independently of human perception.

Operationalization: This process defines the variables of the research for measurement in a more concrete way than conceptualization.

Ordinal: A list of answers that are distinct and can be put in rank order.

Panel Study: In this type of longitudinal study, data are collected with the same people over time.

Participant Observation: This approach to data collection involves the participation and/or observation of the researcher in the community being studied.

Periodicity: This reflects a concern that selecting research subjects through a particular interval may result in a sample that would not be reflective of the broader population. For example, studying prime-time television every seventh evening may result in a sample of Friday evening shows, not reflective of the spectrum of broadcasts throughout the week.

Population: The group of people or artifacts that is the subject of the research. This may or may not be the same group as the study sample, depending on how participants are selected.

Precision: This assessment of variable measurement refers to the number of categories used, with more categories offering potentially more precise observations.

Probability Sampling: These selection processes are used to select the specific subjects of the research based on a sense of the population, such that each subject selected has an equal or known probability for selection. This also can be referred to as random selection procedures.

Purposive Sampling: This non-random process involves selecting research subjects based on an intention to represent designated types.

Quasi-experimental Design: With this design, comparisons are made over time or across groups, but the selection of subjects into groups is not determined through random selection procedures.

Quota Sampling: This non-random process involves selecting subjects to fill designated proportions of particular types.

Random Sampling: This process involves selecting subjects from a group such that each has an equal or known change of being selected for study. See **Probability Sampling.**

Ratio: This level of measurement assumes similar qualities as nominal (attributes are distinct), ordinal (rank-ordered), and interval (with equal distances) but also includes a known zero. Income would be an example.

Reliability: This quality of measurement suggests consistency across observations.

Research access: The availability of research subjects to the people conducting the research.

Research community: A network of professionals engaged in the production, dissemination, and interpretation of research.

Research design: The structure of the research approach, whether observing one case or comparing cases over space or time.

Research documentation: The process of recording observations, such as through paper, computer, audiotape, or video.

Research funding: Fiscal support awarded to specific research projects.

Research implementation: The process of conducting research, including the conceptualization of key ideas, selecting and observing research subjects, and analyzing data.

Research institutions: Agencies engaged in the production, implementation, dissemination, and interpretation of research.

Research justification: Explanations given as to the importance of the research process, in terms of its social and political significance as well as its lack of full exploration within a research community.

Research Purpose: The reason for research can be justified as exploratory, descriptive, or explanatory. Explanatory research involves comparative assessment, whereas exploratory and descriptive research can rely on case study designs.

Research questions: Queries posed at broad, intermediate, and specific levels that guide the direction of the research process.

Research subject: The focus of the research process.

Sample: The actual pool of people or things observed for the study (see **Population**).

Sample bias: This reflects a concern that the research sample is not typical of the broader population it is meant to reflect

Selection: This threat to internal validity affects designs that use comparisons at one point in time, when groups are not randomly assigned.

Snowball Sampling: In this non-random sampling strategy, the researchers first contact key informants, who then suggest additional people for research.

Social Artifact: A concrete manifestation of human action, such as a film or wall graffiti.

Statistical Significance: This empirical significance refers to the degree of possibility that observed results might be a result of sampling error; the degree of acceptability in these numbers is established through conventions among researchers.

Stratified sampling: A probability approach to selecting research subjects using known groups.

Strength: This statistic is used in analyses of two or more variables to assess the degree of difference established in findings.

Subjectivity: An approach to understanding reality that assumes knowledge is based on individual human perception.

Symbolic Value: Numbers may have value in allowing groups to establish identity and visibility.

Systematic sampling: A probability approach to selection based on a known set of research subjects, using a random number to begin and then proceeding with selection based on a known interval.

Testing: This internal threat to validity concerns longitudinal designs, when people are changing over time because they become familiar and conditioned to the tests rather than due to the subject of the study.

Trend Study: This longitudinal design assesses people or conditions over time.

Validity: This can refer to concerns with design, generalization, or measurement. See **External Validity**, **Internal Validity**, and **Measurement Validity**.

Variable: Defined through operationalization; used to organize groups of attributes. In analysis, the variable should represent a condition that varies across observations.

REFERENCES

Allen, M., Emmers, T., Gebhardt, L., & Giery, M. A. (1995). Exposure to pornography and acceptance of rape myths. *Journal of Communication, 45*(1), 5–26.

Allied Media Corporation. (2006). *Arab American.* http://www.allied-media.com/ Arab-American/default.htm. Retrieved April 10, 2006.

Appadurai, A. (1996). *Modernity at large: Cultural dimensions of globalization.* Minneapolis: University of Minnesota Press.

Arab American Institute Foundation (2005). Quick facts about Arab Americans. www.aaiusa.org. Retrieved April 10, 2006.

Associated Press (AP) (2006a). Poll: Most unhappy about search-engine record-keeping. February 24. http://www.foxnews.com/printer_friendly_ story/0,3566,15980,00.html. Retrieved April 6, 2006.

AP (2006b). Poll: Control of TV content up to viewers. March 31. http://www. foxnews.com/story/0,2933,190002,00.html. Retrieved April 15, 2008.

AP (2008). Poll: One in ten get Obama's religion wrong. March 27. http://news. yahoo.com/s/ap/20080327/ap_on_el_pr/obama_muslim_myth_poll. Retrieved April 1, 2008.

Babbie, E. (2004). *The practice of social research,* 10th ed. Belmont, CA: Wadsworth.

Basile, K., Chen, J., Black, M. C., & Saltzman, L. E. (2007). Prevalance and characteristics of sexual violence victimization among U.S. adults 2001–2003. *Criminal Justice Policy Review, 18*(2), 168–199.

Best, J. (2001). *Damned lies and statistics: Untangling numbers from the media, politicians, and activists.* Berkeley: University of California Press.

Black, D., Gates, G., Sanders, S., & Taylor, L. (2007). *The measurement of same-sex unmarried partner couples in the 2000 U.S. Census*. California Center for Population Research. UCLA. Working Paper Series. CCPR-023-07.

Blumenstyck, G. (Oct. 31, 2003). The story of Syngenta & Tyrone Hayes at UC Berkeley: The price of research. *The Chronicle of Higher Education, 50*(10). http://www.mindfully.org/Pesticide/2003/Syngenta-Tyrone-Hayes31oct03.htm. Retrieved April 12, 2008.

Brittingham, A., & de la Cruz, G. P. (March 2005). *We the People of Arab Ancestry in the United States: Census 2000 Special Reports*. Washington DC: U.S. Census Bureau.

Burt, M. (1980). Cultural myths and supports for rape. *Journal of Personality and Social Psychology, 38*, 202–216.

Busby, G. (2006). *Survey: Homeless numbers have risen*. Washington DC: National Policy and Advocacy Council on Homelessness.

Bushman, B. J., & Anderson, C. A. (2001). Media violence and the American public: Scientific facts versus media misinformation. *American Psychologist, 56*(6/7), 477–489.

Campbell, D. (1988). *Methodology and epistemology for social science*. Chicago: University of Chicago Press.

Chang, K. (Aug. 25, 2005). In explaining life's complexity, Darwinists and doubters clash. *New York Times*. www.nytimes.com. Retrieved April 26, 2006.

Chicago Council on Foreign Relations (2002). *American public opinion and U.S. foreign policy*. Chicago: MacArthur Foundation & McCormick Tribune Foundation.

Cho, J., & McLeod, D. M. (2007). Structural antecedents to knowledge and participation: Extending the knowledge gap concept to participation. *Journal of Communication, 57*(2), 205–228.

Chrisafis, A. (March 23, 2009). French Plan to break taboo on ethnic data causes uproar. *The Guardian*. www.guardian.co/uk. Retrieved March 25, 2009.

Clough, A., & Conigrave, K. (2008). Managing confidentiality in illicit drugs research: ethical and legal lessons from studies in remote Aboriginal communities. *Internal Medicine Journal, 38*(1), 60–63.

Cohen, J. (2008). What I watch and who I am: National pride and the viewing of local and foreign television in Israel. *Journal of Communication, 58*(1), 149–167.

Crisp, J. (2003). Refugees and the global politics of asylum. *Political Quarterly*, 75–87.

Data360. (2009). *Global Internet usage*. http://www.data360.org/graph_group. aspx?graph_group_Id=315. Retrieved May 26, 2009.

DeNavas-Walt, C., Proctor, B. D., & Lee, C. H. (2005). *Income, poverty, and health insurance coverage in the United States: 2005*. U.S. Government Printing Office, Washington DC: U.S. Census Bureau.

Dixon, T. (2008). Crime news and racialized beliefs: Understanding the relationship between local news viewing and perceptions of African Americans and crime. *Journal of Communication, 58*(1), 106–125.

Drever, A. (1999). *Homeless count methodologies: An annotated bibliography.* Institute for the Study of Homelessness and Poverty.

Emigh, R. J. (2002). Numeracy or enumeration? The uses of numbers by states and societies. *Social Science History, 26*(4), 653–698.

Farrell, S. J., & Reissing, E. D. (2004). Picking up the challenge: Development of a methodology to enumerate and assess the needs of the street homeless population. *Evaluation Review, 28,* 144–155.

Gallup. (2006). *Questionnaire profile. Gallup poll social series: Lifestyle.* Retrieved April 6, 2006, from: http://brain.gallup.com/documents/questionnaire.

Gandy, O. (2010). *Coming to terms with change: Engaging rational discrimination and cumulative disadvantage.* Burlington, VT: Ashgate.

Goodstein, L. (Oct. 19, 2005). Witness defends broad definition of science. *New York Times.* www.nytimes.com. Retrieved April 26, 2006.

Hetsroni, A. (2007). Three decades of sexual content on prime-time network programming: A longitudinal meta-analytic review. *Journal of Communication, 57*(2), 318–348.

Hornik, R., & McAnany, E. (2001). Theories and evidence: Mass media effects and fertility change. *Communication Theory, 11,* 454–471.

Humphreys, L. (1970). *Tearoom trade: Impersonalized sex in public places.* Chicago: Aldine.

Iganski, P. (2007). Too few Jews to count? Police monitoring of hate crime against Jews in the United Kingdom. *American Behavioral Scientist,* October, 232–245.

Inside Higher Ed. (March 27, 2008). *Faculty are liberal—who cares?* http://www.insidehighered.com/news/2008/03/27/politics. Retrieved April 1, 2008.

Jensen, R. (2007). *Getting off: Pornography and the end of masculinity.* Boston: South End Press.

Johns Hopkins University School of Public Health. (2006). *Updated Iraq survey affirms earlier mortality estimates.* http://www.jhsph.edu/publichealthnews/press_release/2006/burnham_iraq_2006.html. Retrieved October 11, 2006.

Jordan, A. (1992). Social class, temporal orientation, and mass media use within the family system. *Critical Studies in Mass Communication, 9*(4), 374–386.

Kovaleski, S. F., & Chan, W. (Feb. 16, 2001). Indicators show D.C. homelessness getting worse: Service provider reports at odds with official estimates. *Washington Post.*

Kuhn, T. (1970). *The structure of scientific revolutions.* Chicago: University of Chicago Press.

Maio, G. (2002). The cultural specificity of research ethics—or why ethical debate in France is different. *Journal of Medical Ethics, 28,* 147–150.

McMurtrie, B. (May 9, 2003). Refuge for the persecuted: Group finds temporary havens for academics who are in danger in their home countries. *Chronicle of Higher Education, 49*(35), A40.

Milgram, S. (1965). Some conditions of obedience and disobedience to authority. *Human Relations, 18,* 47–68.

Mitchell, T. (1991). America's Egypt: Discourse of the development industry. *Middle East Report, 21*(2), 18–34.

Monaghan, P. (Sept. 1, 1993). Sociologist spends 16 weeks in Spokane County Jail. *Chronicle of Higher Education.*

Murray, M. (2005). *Bush, GOP mired in political quicksand.* NBC News. http://www.msnbc.msn.com/id/9981177. Retrieved April 4, 2006.

National Coalition for the Homeless (NCH) (2005). *How many people experience homelessness?* NCH fact sheet #2. Washington DC: National Coalition for the Homeless.

National Organization for Research at the University of Chicago (NORC) (2003). *Resident relocation survey methodology and results.*

Niederdeppe, J., Davis, K. C., Farrelly, M. C., & Yarsevich, J. (2007). Stylistic features, need for sensation, and confirmed recall of national smoking prevention advertisements. *Journal of Communication, 57*(2), 272–292.

Nyiri, Z. (2007). European Muslims show no conflict between religious and national identities. *Gallup World Poll.* http://www.muslimwestfacts.com/mwf/105931/European-Muslims-Show-Conflict-Between-Religious-National-Identities.aspx. Retrieved April 3, 2009.

Orr, H. A. (May 30, 2005). Why intelligent design isn't. *The New Yorker.*

Pew Research Center (March 27, 2008). *Obama weathers the Wright Storm, Clinton faces credibility problem.* http://pewresearch.org/pubs/779/obama-weathers-the-wright-storm-clinton-faces-credibility-problem. Retrieved April 1, 2008.

Pew Research Center for the People and the Press (2005). *Mid-September 2005 political survey: Final questionnaire.*

Phan, K. (Feb. 25, 2009). Texas study claims school districts 'rob' students of sex ed. *Christian Post.* www.christianpost.com. Retrieved April 3, 2009.

Pittenger, D. J. (2003). Internet research: An opportunity to revisit classic ethical problems in behavioral research. *Ethics & Behavior, 13*(1), 45–60.

Polling Report. (2009). *Iraq.* www.pollingreport.com/iraq.htm. Retrieved March 24, 2009.

Popper, K. (1959). *The logic of scientific discovery.* New York: Harper & Row.

Quindlen, A. (March 16, 2009). Let's talk about sex: Congress loves abstinence-only programs so much it has thrown big bucks at them. The public? It's got better ideas. *Newsweek,* p. 62.

Robbin, A. (2000). The politics of representation in the U.S. national statistical system: origins of minority population interest group participation. *Journal of Government Information, 27,* 431–453.

Rorty, R. (1993). *A world without intrinsic properties.* Speech presented to the Chinese University of Hong Kong.

Rossouw, H. (May 3, 2002). A sociologist in the Congo struggles to recover from jail. *Chronicle of Higher Education,* p. A41.

Said, E. (1978). *Orientalism.* New York: Pantheon Books.

Salaita, S. (2005). Ethnic identity and imperative patriotism: Arab Americans before and after 9/11. *College Literature, 32*(2), 146–169.

Santellis, J. S., & Kantor, L. A. (2008). Introduction to special issue: Human rights, cultural, and scientific aspects of abstinence-only policies and programs. *Sexuality Research & Social Policy, 5*(3), 1–5.

Schüklenk, U. (2000). Protecting the vulnerable: testing times for clinical research ethics. *Social Science & Medicine, 51*(6), 969–977.

Sternberg, S. (April 1, 2009). Cardiologists examine conflicts of interest with drug-makers; Take-away message: Reform needed now. *USA Today*, p. 10B.

Strobel, W. P., & Landay, J. S. (Nov. 12, 2005). Operatives don't back CIA torture exemption. *Austin American Statesman*, p. A15.

Taylor, R. J., & Lincoln, K. D. (1997). *The Million Man March: Portraits and attitudes*. www.rcgd.isr.umich.edu/prba/perspectives/winter1997/rtaylor1.pdf. Retrieved April 12, 2008.

Urla, J. (1993). Cultural politics in an age of statistics: Numbers, nations, and the making of Basque identity. *American Ethnologist, 20*(4), 818–843.

U.S. Census (2000). *Individual census report*. Washington DC: U.S. Department of Commerce Bureau of Census.

U.S. Department of Housing and Urban Development (2004*). HUD's homeless assistance programs: A guide to counting unsheltered homeless people*.

Wilkins, K. (2004). The Civil Intifada: Power and politics of the Palestinian census. *Development & Change, 35*(5), 891–908.

Wittgenstein, L. (1958). *Philosophical investigations* (G.E.M. Anscombe, Trans.). New York: MacMillan Press.

World Bank (2009). *Atlas of Global Development*. Washington DC: World Bank.

Yick, A. (2007). Role of culture and context: ethical issues in research with Asian Americans and immigrants in intimate violence. *Journal of Family Violence, 22*(5), 277–285.

Zuberi, T. (2001). *Thicker than blood: How racial statistics lie*. Minneapolis: University of Minnesota Press.

INDEX

....

A

ABC, 20
Aboriginal community, 67
Action research, 69
Africa, 77–78
African-American community,
    45, 79
Alaska, 67
Alternative explanations, 80–82
American Association for Public
    Opinion Research, 15
American community, 50
American Conservative Union, 21
American Medical
    Association, 84
American Psychological
    Association, 84
American Sociological
    Association, 17, 67
Animal rights movement, 67
Anomie, 48
Anonymity, 59–61, 64–67, 69

Anti-semitism, 68
Arab community, 45
Arab-American community, 18
Asia, 75
Asian community, 45
Assent, 64
Atrazine, 21
Attrition, 28–30
Australia, 17, 67

B

Basque community, 8, 49
Berlin, 75–76
Best, J., xii
Bivariate Analysis, 74

C

Caribbean, 76–77
Case study design, x, 25, 30–34,
    82, 88
Causality, xi, 27, 33, 80
Caucasian community, 58–59